"YOU'RE IN THE WRONG BATHROOM!"

"YOU'RE IN THE WRONG BATHROOM!"

And 20 Other Myths
and Misconceptions
About Transgender and
Gender-Nonconforming
People

LAURA ERICKSON-SCHROTH, MD
LAURA A. JACOBS, LCSW-R

BEACON PRESS
BOSTON

Beacon Press
Boston, Massachusetts
www.beacon.org

Beacon Press books
are published under the auspices of
the Unitarian Universalist Association of Congregations.

20 19 18 17   8 7 6 5 4 3 2 1

This book is printed on acid-free paper that meets the uncoated paper
ANSI/NISO specifications for permanence as revised in 1992.

Text design and composition by Kim Arney

Library of Congress Cataloging-in-Publication Data

Names: Erickson-Schroth, Laura, author. | Jacobs, Laura A. (Clinical social
    work/therapist), author.
Title: "You're in the wrong bathroom!" : and 20 other myths and
    misconceptions about transgender and gender-nonconforming people / Laura
    Erickson-Schroth, MD, Laura A. Jacobs, LCSW-R.
Description: Boston : Beacon Press, [2017] | Includes bibliographical
    references.
Identifiers: LCCN 2016055090 | ISBN 9780807033890 (pbk. : alk. paper)
Subjects: LCSH: Transgender people. | Transgenderism. | Sexual minorities.
Classification: LCC HQ77.9 .E74 2017 | DDC 306.76/8—dc23
LC record available at https://lccn.loc.gov/2016055090

CONTENTS

"YOU'RE IN THE WRONG BATHROOM!"

PART 1

IDENTITY

You've Never Met a Transgender Person

There are approximately one million transgender people in the United States, and chances are you've met one (or more) of them. So why do so many people assume they haven't?

To answer this question, we have to go back to the 1960s, when researchers first made estimates of the prevalence of transgender populations. Transgender people (known as "transsexual" at the time) were just beginning to be recognized and to see themselves in the news media. In 1952, Christine Jorgensen, a World War II veteran, had returned home from a gender-affirming surgery in Denmark to the New York *Daily News* front-page coverage of her story: "Ex-GI Becomes Blonde Beauty." Jorgensen was better known, but others had undergone similar surgeries, including Lili Elbe, whose story was the subject of the 2015 movie *The Danish Girl*, in 1930.

In the wake of these early surgeries and the public interest they garnered, medical professionals attempted to estimate the prevalence of transgender people, but had little information to work with. The only reliable statistics were based on the number of people who had undergone gender-affirming surgeries. However, most transgender people were not having surgery, and many were living marginalized lives, obtaining hormones via black-market sources, or, for the most part, were simply people assigned male at birth but living full time as female with no access to formal treatments, including surgeries. There were an infinite number of reasons for this, including cost, subpar results, and the profound bravery it took to come out as transgender. Still, physicians reported their results at conferences around the world, and numbers started to circulate. They were in the range of one in thirty thousand to one in one hundred thousand people.

Statistics from the early 1970s seemed to show that it was more common to be a transgender woman (someone who is assigned male at birth and identifies as a woman) than a transgender man (someone who is assigned female at birth and identifies as a man). Researchers came up with numerous theories to explain this discrepancy, including biological reasons and social explanations. For example, some argued that people assigned female at birth were given more leeway in their clothing and social roles (women could wear pants, but men couldn't wear dresses) and so felt less of a need to transition. What the researchers didn't consider, but which probably contributed significantly to the differences in rates, was that surgeries for transgender women were more advanced than those for transgender men, so more trans women than men were presenting for surgery.

Transgender men were not the only people missing from the statistics. Because surgery was expensive, people from lower socioeconomic classes were less likely to end up in clinics. White transgender people were also overrepresented due to racial discrimination.

In a time before the rapid communication of cell phones and computers, when transgender support groups were unheard of, it was extremely difficult to gather better statistics than these. The problem is that as transgender communities grew, and these numbers were obviously inaccurate, there was little impetus to correct or update them. As a result, these early numbers continued to be quoted in major US newspapers and magazines into the 2000s.

A well-known and respected report published in 2011 by the Williams Institute estimates that transgender people comprise about 0.3 percent of the US population, or approximately 1 in every 333 people. These more accurate numbers come both from up-to-date estimates of the number of people who undergo some kind of medical transition and from population-based studies in which people, regardless of whether they have physically transitioned, are given a chance to define themselves.

Over time, as more current statistics circulate, it has become apparent that transgender people are not as rare as was once thought. However, there are reasons other than inaccurate statistics driving our collective sense that we don't know anyone transgender.

Would you recognize someone as transgender if that person didn't tell you? Most people think they would. But they would be wrong. Many transgender people live "stealth," at least to the general public, telling only those they are close to about their identities. For centuries, long before hormone therapies or gender-reassignment surgeries, there were people whose cross-gendered lives were not known until their deaths. For instance, more than two hundred people assigned female at birth are thought to have fought as men in the Civil War. Some were women, but some were transgender men. Billy Tipton, a jazz musician popular in the 1940s and 1950s, and the inspiration for the 1998 novel *Trumpet*, lived his life as a man despite being assigned female at birth and kept his birth-assigned gender secret, even to his own son. Today, thousands of transgender Americans go about their lives with few people knowing that they are transgender.

There are physical attributes that make it easier and harder to "pass" as cisgender, another word for nontransgender people. In many instances, transgender men have an advantage because testosterone leads to changes like increased musculature, growth of body and facial hair, and a deepening voice, all of which signal masculinity. For this reason, it is often more difficult for transgender women to avoid being "read" as transgender once they have gone through a male-typical puberty. Trans women are often, though not always, taller than the average woman, with sharper jaw lines, deeper

voices, Adam's apples, and facial hair. These features can be difficult to change. In some instances, transgender people do not want to
change them and may feel comfortable in their bodies the way they
are. Others want very much to physically transition but cannot afford surgical interventions. "Passing" is a controversial topic within
transgender communities. Outsiders often judge transgender people by their ability to "pass" as cisgender, but so do some transgender people. This leads to hierarchies and discrimination within
transgender communities.

The belief that transgender people are recognizably distinct from
nontransgender people assumes that there is something we can pick
out about a transgender person's clothing, body shape, or speech
that "gives them away." It assumes that trans people never escape
their "essential" gender assigned at birth—that they are never "really" a part of the gender with which they identify.

Why do we have this belief? What purpose does it serve? For one
thing, it helps us to feel secure that we will not be "tricked" about
someone's gender. But why is it so important to us that we are not
"tricked?" Some might argue that it is about genitals—that we want
to know the genital status of the people we are going on a date with
or going to the bathroom with. But why would—or should—we care
about the genital status of people in the checkout line with us at the
grocery store or in the seat across from us on the train?

Clearly the concern is not just about genitals; it's also about
gender. We have a lot of expectations about people based on their
gender. We regulate the way boys and girls, men and women work,
play, dress, and love each other. And if someone doesn't fit into
one of our gender categories, we're not sure what to expect of them
and may sometimes find ourselves upset. Transgender people are
harassed, discriminated against, and all-too-often assaulted or
murdered. Stepping outside of gender boundaries can provoke
significant hostility. It's crucial to ask ourselves why it bothers us
so much to see these lines blurred.

Another reason many of us may assume we've never met a transgender person is that we imagine trans people are unlikely to be involved in the same activities or groups that we are. But there are trans people of every ethnicity, religion, socioeconomic status, and profession. They include filmmaker Lana Wachowski, actress Laverne Cox, US Olympian Chris Mosier, Pennsylvania physician general Rachel Levine, Orthodox Jewish professor Joy Ladin, writer Kate Bornstein, comedian Ian Harvie, activist Jamison Green, and billionaire Jennifer Pritzker, among numerous others.

Trans people have written in just about every genre there is, and many have published personal stories. There are first-hand accounts by trans men (*Nina Here Nor There*, Nick Krieger), trans women (*Redefining Realness*, Janet Mock), and trans teens (*Some Assembly Required*, Arin Andrews). There are anthologies that tell multiple stories (*Gender Outlaws: The Next Generation*, Kate Bornstein and S. Bear Bergman). There are also a whole host of TV shows (*Transparent*), feature films (*Gun Hill Road*), and documentaries (*Southern Comfort*) depicting the lives of trans people. Nonprofit organizations (the Sylvia Rivera Law Project) do advocacy work related to transgender communities, and conferences (Philadelphia Transgender Health Conference) provide spaces for trans and nontrans people to meet. Any of these can be first steps to learning more about transgender people.

All Trans People Want to Be Either Barbie or Ken

Barbie and Ken . . . tiny figurines that pack such a cultural punch. These eleven-inch plastic dolls, generally a light shade of pink with hands, feet, arms, legs, heads, and torsos all in the rough shapes of a genuine human body, have an endless array of accessories. They drive convertibles and live in large, well-furnished homes. Their faces are frozen in perpetual smiles, and they seem carefree.

Until very recently Barbie had always been portrayed as a tall, slender, feminine, Caucasian debutante in cocktail dresses, stilettos, and perfect, in-season couture bags, or perhaps in crisp pink miniskirts, or even in form-fitting swimsuits that accentuated her narrow hips and ample breasts. She sported weightless blonde hair, eyes the blue of the Pacific, and nails that sparkled in fire-engine red. Her blush and lipstick were flawless from sunrise to sunset, and she hosted parties for the elite. She was every little girl's dream.

Barbie's eternal partner, Ken, was always unmistakably masculine, a Caucasian, preppy college student in polo shirts and loafers. He was an expert with a tennis racket and a confident, yet sensitive, boyfriend who never forgot to bring flowers. The debutante's ideal mate.

GI Joe, an "action figure," was similarly ideal, representing hypermasculinity as a musclebound, uniformed, no-nonsense soldier in military fatigues and combat boots. His gun and "kung fu grip" were extremes of authoritative power, and as a toy targeted to adolescent and preadolescent boys, his overall demeanor was replete with male virility.

These toys represent ideals of gender and of lifestyle: extremes of femininity and masculinity as defined by Western, twentieth- and twenty-first-century cultural norms, expressing middle-class Caucasian American fantasies of what women and men should be. Originally encoded within Barbie was the notion of a job-free or homemaker existence for women, while Ken still portrayed the stable, usually white-collar-destined college graduate and GI Joe, the lifelong military man. Taken together, Barbie and Ken represent a relationship of Caucasian, heterosexual monogamy, standard forms of dress, and a life of means, with style, friendship, and happiness. All three model polarized images of gender and an explicit gender binary—that is, the idea that there are only two genders, male and female, each distinct from the other—as well as assumptions about career, class, conformity, attractiveness, race, ability/disability, and sexuality. These images are so ubiquitous in Western societies that we have internalized them, but their influence on our understandings of gender and sexual orientation cannot be underestimated.

To address some of these issues, Mattel expanded the Barbie line in early 2016 to be more inclusive of diversity, and today, Barbies can be purchased in a variety of body types, skin colorings, and ethnicities. In addition, career-oriented Barbies have been available for some time. But the classic Barbie and Ken, along with their socially conforming identities, remain in the consciousness of so many.

Still, many youths "queered" both toys, and in private play, away from parental oversight, the figurines provided safe preadolescent titillation in ways that were definitely *not* Mattel-approved. Business Ken/GI Joe was a popular combination: children often invented scenes in which the two attractive gentlemen crept into shadowy, hidden spaces to exchange forbidden pleasure; meanwhile, countless Barbies in frilly pink bedrooms engaged in femme-femme lesbian trysts whose passion might only be captured in Sapphic poetry. Their exploratory play remained secret until outed by Erica Rand in *Barbie's Queer Accessories*.

Many see Barbie and Ken as images of idealized genders that transgender people might aspire to. Well-known transgender people visible on television and in the media, such as Caitlyn Jenner, Janet Mock, and Chaz Bono, at least on the surface appear to emulate classic expressions of gender, wearing designer clothes and jetsetting from mansion to elite hotel to television show or award appearance in limos. These individuals are often protrayed in mainstream media as though they were to be role models, giving the impression that everyone in the trans community should follow their examples.

Western culture also praises and rewards transgender people who match cultural ideals for how feminine or masculine they appear. It's not uncommon for a trans person to hear attempted compliments such as "I would never have known" or "You look so good [as a man/woman]." Some people call this "passing": the ability to move through the world as one's post-transition gender with one's transness going unnoticed. The ability to be seen as "natural" (i.e., assigned your post-transition gender at birth) carries a privilege not available to all, and people who pass are less likely to generate hostility in public. But many trans people are unsure how to interpret these "compliments." Is passing somehow better? Is someone who doesn't pass of less value?

That said, it is also true that many people in trans communities feel that something in these gender ideals is authentic for them. They may dress as male or female in ways that are clear and unmistakable, and feel very natural doing so.

But are these stereotyped genders what *every* trans person wants?

Not exactly. While these ideals fit some, others in transgender and gender-nonconforming communities find these stereotypes to be artificial or offensive. Many critiques of Barbie and Ken have described how the dolls feature proportions that are unattainable in actual human bodies. Some have suggested that the exaggerated waist and breasts of Barbies before the recent introduction of body-diverse dolls are unhealthy and unreasonable for any woman to meet and that Barbie's appearance, styling, and often helpless, vapid demeanor seem tailored toward male desire. Ken and GI Joe are similarly unnaturally perfect, with physiques requiring countless hours in a gym. Joe is inalterably authoritative and stern, while Ken is masculine yet sympathetic, never angry nor inattentive. None of the three seems fully "real."

Large numbers of trans people do not feel these expressions of gender are authentic to their transitions. While extremes are not right or wrong, many within trans communities view gender as a spectrum from female to male, a rainbow from Barbie to GI Joe, with countless hues between and themselves somewhere in the middle.

Additionally, transgender and gender-nonconforming people rarely have bodies that match the artificial proportions of these dolls; many are not Caucasian; and Barbie and Ken have always had access to financial privilege otherwise available to relatively few.

The way trans people see their identities is complicated and is influenced by historical circumstances. For most of the twentieth century, trans people were expected to adhere closely to social norms of gender and to identify as heterosexual in their post-transition gender in order to be eligible for services such as hormone therapy and surgeries. For some, these stories were authentic, but others, desperate for care, simply repeated what they knew doctors wanted to hear. Early versions of the Standards of Care, published by the World Professional Association for Transgender Health (WPATH, previously known as the Harry Benjamin International Gender Dysphoria Association), required binary presentations, and consensus among early providers like Harry Benjamin was that the only way for transgender people to survive in society was for them to blend in as seamlessly as possible. This limited transition to just a few, and at Johns Hopkins University, the most well-known gender service in the country, two thousand people applied for services and just twenty-four were allowed to surgically transition prior to the program's closing in 1979.

Only over time did the trans community, and the LGBTQ+ community more broadly, confront these restrictive programs and create opportunities for members to live in other ways. Progress has been made in medical and mental health communities as well. Version six of the WPATH Standards of Care, published in 2001, acknowledged an openness to identities outside the gender binary. Version seven, published in 2014, very directly accepts a multiplicity of genders and encourages aiding people whose identities fall outside binary social norms, though some providers even now enforce earlier, outdated and strict interpretations.

Today, anything is possible. "Trans" comes in countless varieties, and associated with each different form of transness are terms used to describe who individuals understand themselves to be. The language can be extremely personal and can carry a great deal of meaning about identity. People usually have specific reasons they prefer one term over another. Sometimes terms have similar or overlapping meanings, and definitions depend on who you ask. It is polite to refer to trans people by their self-identified gender (who they feel themselves to be) and by their post-transition gender (the gender they are after their transition), unless they specifically request otherwise. The best bet is to ask what they prefer.

But here are a few generalities:

Some people simply see themselves as male or female and use the terms "man" or "woman" to refer to the gender they understand themselves to be or to have become. They often completely reject the gender they were assigned at birth and may live stealth. These people tend to dress in ways that match the norms we usually see in society and in the media.

"Transgender" and "trans" are often used as umbrella terms to describe a wide range of transgender and gender-nonconforming people, and they don't necessarily indicate anything about how individuals might express themselves.

Some people use terms such as "transmasculine" or "trans man" (someone who has become or understands himself as a man) and "transfeminine" or "trans woman" (someone who has become or understands herself as a woman); each of these attempts to incorporate one's transness into a gender label. Others describe themselves as men or women "of trans experience," making clear they *are* male or female, while also acknowledging their trans past. Again, unless someone asks for a different label, it is respectful to refer to people according to their post-transition gender.

Increasingly, many people have different understandings of what it means to be male or female, and may feel themselves to be outside gender binaries altogether. The terms used by these people can be more complex and might be confusing to the uninitiated.

The phrases "gender nonconforming" and "transgender and gender nonconforming" (often abbreviated as TGNC) are umbrella terms for those not identifying in binary male/female ways. This is an attempt to be inclusive of people who transition but may not look or think of themselves as one gender or the other. They often dress in ways that incorporate a variety of genders or indicate no gender at all.

Some people find the term "nonconforming" to be negative, implying that there are standards some people live up to and others don't. Instead, some use "gender expansive" to capture the feeling of expanding the realms of gender in groundbreaking ways.

"Genderqueer" is a term that can have two different but related meanings. Some use it to explain that their gender is more complex than simply male or female, and that it lies somewhere on a spectrum between these. For others, "genderqueer" has political significance. People who see it this way may feel that they are "queering" gender;

that is, they express themselves in ways that play with gender, problematize it, and they actively confront social norms of gender so as to force outsiders to consider the gender stereotypes active within culture. For example, genderqueer trans men may wear cosmetics and genderqueer trans women may wear ties. By being provocative and making their gender an unavoidable topic, they hope to open up the possibilities of gender.

"Genderfluid" is also an increasingly common term and can reflect a person's feeling that their gender shifts from day to day along a continuum. They may feel internally or express themselves more masculinely one day, more femininely the next, and androgynously at other points.

Similarly, "demigender" (half-gender) is used to denote people who feel they have a partial connection to a certain gender (i.e., demiboy or demigirl), while "bigender" (two-gender) refers to someone who incorporates both. "Two Spirit" is a Native American term also referring to a person whose gender is a combination of both male and female. Some feel that this term should be used only by people of Native American descent, as it carries cultural connotations and could be considered appropriation if used by others.

"Agender" (non-gender) expresses the idea that while someone's physical body might align more with male or female, the person's actual identity is without gender altogether.

And some joyously call themselves "gender unicorns"—rare and fantastical creatures who might seemingly defy the laws of nature and cannot exist, yet do.

Each term means something different to each person and reflects the fact that people in transgender communities have a wide range of ways of understanding themselves.

In the end, no gender identity or presentation is any more legitimate than any other. Society is expanding how it thinks of gender, and our culture is becoming more inclusive of all the gender possibilities.

Barbie and Ken are just as valid as the most extreme, genderqueer, outside-the-box gender expression. Some gender identities may make it easier to exist within society, but none is inherently better.

In the end, the only gender that is right for someone is the one that person chooses.

You're Not Really Trans If You Haven't Had "the Surgery"

"She's transitioning? Has she had 'the surgery' yet?"

This is one of the most common questions transgender people get. Many nontrans people assume that genital surgery is the ultimate goal of transitioning. Yet within transgender communities there is significant diversity as to people's desire for surgery and, if they want it, what kind. When people outside transgender communities talk about surgery, they often mean genital surgery. However, there are all kinds of gender-affirming surgeries, including breast augmentation, "top" surgery (to create a male-contoured chest), and facial feminization surgeries. Contrary to popular belief, many trans people never have "bottom" or genital surgery. Transgender men, for example, are much more likely to have chest reconstruction than genital surgery.

Trans people's desires for surgery are a reflection of the diversity of gender identities in trans communities. Some people, particularly those who identify as genderqueer, feel most comfortable appearing androgynous, and they may take low-dose hormones or have top surgery with the goal of looking somewhere between male and female. The decision to have (or not have) a particular surgery is often related to people's identity and what they feel will make them most comfortable.

There are numerous reasons trans people may or may not choose a particular surgery. Some surgeries cost tens of thousands of dollars, and, historically, most employer-sponsored health plans and state Medicaid plans have specifically excluded transition-related health care, forcing people to pay for hormones and surgeries out of pocket. This is close to impossible for low-income people and difficult for many in the middle class. Even for those whose employer-sponsored or state Medicaid programs do purport to pay for gender-affirming surgeries, the amount that the insurance company or state pays may be lower than some surgeons are willing to accept, either because surgeons are trying to make a significant profit or, in some instances, because surgeons are not even sure they can break even after paying the operating room and staff expenses.

Some people forgo or delay surgery to maintain relationships with partners or family members who oppose it. Sexual functioning can also play a role in some people's decisions. Though, in recent years, improved surgical techniques have enabled people to enjoy satisfying sexual functioning, many people still choose to retain their original parts and continue to use them.

An overlooked consideration of surgery is its effect on personal safety. Some trans women, for example, prioritize facial feminization surgery because it can improve their ability to move through the world as female, with less fear of being subject to ridicule and violence.

There are also many systemic barriers that can make it difficult for trans people to access surgeries. For certain procedures, there are few well-trained surgeons here in the United States and abroad. Trans women interested in vaginoplasty, or trans men seeking phalloplasty, often end up flying to see the handful of surgeons with good reputations; some people travel outside the United States, commonly to Thailand or Mexico, where there are also expertly trained surgeons. Unfortunately, many surgeons, here and abroad, practice techniques that are out of date or dangerous, and it can be hard to tell the difference between good and bad doctors without doing extensive research.

Traveling far from home for surgery, whether within the United States or overseas, can have other disadvantages. Though some people are able to afford to stay on site for a week or two after a procedure, it can significantly add to the cost to stay in a hotel and possibly to bring a loved one for assistance, making this luxury unattainable for many who must return home, often to areas with little access to quality follow-up care if there are complications. Even when staying in the United States for surgery, many people travel far from home and, because of the expense, may return before they have fully healed.

There is also a backlog for many procedures in the United States, which stems from a dearth of surgeons trained in trans health care. Surgeons working in this area of medicine come from a variety of specialties, including plastic surgery, gynecology, and urology, and there are no clearly defined guidelines or board certifications that make someone eligible to perform transition-related surgeries. In addition, almost no surgical residency programs provide any exposure to transgender care. Surgeons interested in learning how to perform gender-affirming surgeries have traditionally completed short apprenticeships with someone who is already performing these surgeries, but this training involves seeking out mentorship and taking time off from paid work. Because there are few such trained surgeons, and no clear way of vetting those who do exist, it is possible to start a practice doing gender-related surgeries for the sole purpose of making money, without much regard for good technique or outcomes. The quality of surgeons varies greatly. In recent years, some academic medical centers have begun discussing how to start fellowships—additional training after residency—for those who desire to go into transgender surgery. In addition, some organizations, such as the World Professional Association for Transgender Health (WPATH), have taken steps toward creating certification programs for those who provide transgender care.

Surgical options for trans women include facial feminization, tracheal shave, breast augmentation, and genital surgeries (orchiectomy, vaginoplasty). With facial feminization, a plastic surgeon makes changes to areas of the face (forehead, nose, cheeks, lips, jaw, chin) that result in a more feminine-appearing profile. These surgeries are very expensive and, because they are considered "cosmetic," typically not covered by insurance. Yet they may be important—even vital—to a person's day-to-day life as they provide the ability to pass, and therefore greater opportunity to find employment and increased physical safety when moving through the world. A tracheal shave reduces the size of the thyroid cartilage (the Adam's apple), also resulting in a more feminine appearance. Breast augmentation for transgender women is a similar but not identical procedure to breast augmentation in cisgender women. Silicone or saline implants are inserted into the chest, but the placement of the prosthetics may vary slightly due to differing underlying physiology. The World Professional Association for Transgender Health's Standards of Care recommend at least twelve months of hormone treatment before breast augmentation to assess how much breast growth develops prior to surgery.

Orchiectomy is a procedure in which the testicles are removed but the penis remains. There are several reasons someone might choose to have an orchiectomy rather than a vaginoplasty, which is the removal of the testicles and penis and creation of a vagina. Orchiectomies are far less expensive than vaginoplasties (approximately $5,000 versus $30,000), and an orchiectomy may be a first step, prior to vaginoplasty, for someone who cannot yet afford vaginoplasty but would like to stop the production of androgens (masculinizing hormones like testosterone). This can have risks for individuals who would later pursue vaginoplasty, as some argue the penile and scrotal tissue may atrophy, leaving less material for the creation of a vulva and vaginal canal. Others have no intention of proceeding to vaginoplasty and would like to retain their penises but decrease androgen production.

Vaginoplasty is the procedure many people are referring to when they use the phrase "the surgery." It involves removing the testicles and much of the penis (though preserving parts of the penis as the new clitoris) and creating a vaginal canal (typically from penile tissue) and labia (typically from scrotal tissue). Many trans women are pleased with the results of vaginoplasty, which, for such a complex procedure, has low complication rates. The abilities to urinate and orgasm are generally well preserved. Vaginoplasty requires lifetime "maintenance" with dilators to maintain flexibility and depth.

Surgical options for trans men include chest reconstruction and genital surgeries (metoidioplasty, phalloplasty, scrotoplasty). Top surgery is the most common procedure trans men undergo. There is more than one method of top surgery, and the choice is generally based on the size of a person's chest. Smaller-chested people are able to undergo a "keyhole" procedure that removes tissue through an incision in the nipple, resulting in minimal scarring, and larger-chested people undergo a double-incision procedure that removes tissue through incisions under each breast. After top surgery, many trans men enjoy the freedom to go shirtless, especially when swimming. Many people find creative ways to address scarring by allowing their chest hair to grow over scars or getting tattoos.

Genital surgeries for trans men are not as advanced as they are for trans women. One of the most common procedures in the United States is metoidioplasty, in which the length of the clitoris is extended to better represent a penis. This can be done with or without extending the urethra through the new penis so that the man can stand to pee. Metoidioplasty generally does not produce a penis comparable in size to those of cisgender men. Phalloplasty, which is performed infrequently in the United States but is common in countries with national health-care systems that finance it, does create a comparably sized penis, but it has drawbacks. The cost of phalloplasty is high (approximately $100,000), and it frequently involves multiple procedures. A "donor site," often a forearm or thigh, is needed. Skin and tissue below the skin (nerves and blood vessels) are harvested from this site. Phalloplasties can result in numerous complications and often do not allow for erections, though for some people, the appearance of the penis is more important than the ability to produce an erection. Metoidioplasty and phalloplasty are sometimes accompanied by scrotoplasty, which is the creation of scrotum, usually by inserting egg-shaped silicone testicles into reshaped labia.

In spite of the many options for surgeries, the myth that surgery makes a trans person "fully" male or female still circulates. It's not uncommon to hear that a person is "more trans" for desiring surgery, and that those who haven't yet had or cannot afford these changes are "less" trans. Even within trans communities, there are hierarchies set up between those who are "pre-op" (pre-operative), "non-op," and "post-op" (post-operative), often resulting in shame and low self-esteem in those who cannot afford or do not want the surgeries others consider important.

One of the goals that many outside trans communities imagine trans people would prioritize is being able to have sex "normally"— meaning, as a heterosexual person. The notion of becoming heterosexual after transition had been institutionalized in the earlier WPATH Standards of Care and became so inherent in the conversations others have about trans people that cisgender people frequently ask things like "If she wanted to be with women, why didn't she just stay a man?" People wonder why those with a functioning penis would want to lose that organ if they were going to end up sleeping with women. And the reverse: Why would someone who identifies as a woman and is attracted to men not want to have a vaginoplasty so she can have "normal" sex with men? Thinking this way conflates gender identity and sexuality, and devalues sex that is not understood to be traditionally heterosexual.

Surgery is one of many ways in which trans people are judged about how trans they really are. Another is their gender histories. Trans people are generally expected to have understood that they were different early in life (preschool age) and to have discovered their trans identity as children. If they are transitioning as adults, they are presumed to have hidden their secret until they could not stand it anymore. In this scenario, they are assumed to have hated their pre-transition bodies and to enjoy everything about one gender while rejecting everything about the other. This narrative is true for some people, but not for many others. Those who don't feel "different" until later in life, or who don't hate their bodies, or who enjoy things considered both masculine and feminine, are often seen as imposters. For many years, trans people could not access hormones or surgery without providing a familiar narrative, and so some learned to hide their true selves—a fascinating paradox given that transitioning is thought of as the process of revealing your true self.

It is easy to see how the idea of being "complete" or "fully" trans after surgery may make sense to nontrans people; a surgeon makes physical changes to the body that result in a different appearance. But it is crucial to remember that there is so much more to being a man than having a penis, and so much more to being a woman than having a vagina, and that the countless other gender possibilities are no less worthy.

Trans People Are "Trapped in the Wrong Body"

The expression "trapped in the wrong body" is prevalent both in trans communities and in the culture at large, and it informs how so many people think about trans and gender-nonconforming identity. The idea is that there is a mismatch between the gender of a person's physical body and the gender in that person's brain.

The concept of being "trapped in the wrong body" has influenced medical protocols and services provided to transgender people since the 1950s. Medical and mental health providers have based assessment and treatment of trans people on this notion, and many researchers still actively search the body and brain for signs that genetics or hormones lead trans people's brains to be gendered separately from their bodies.

Although it may be popular, not all trans and gender-nonconforming people feel this theory accurately describes them, and to date, there is no conclusive scientific evidence of its validity. Where did this notion come from? How did it become so entrenched? And why are we so attached to the idea that trans identity is not a choice?

The history of "trapped in the wrong body" goes back further than most realize. Karl Ulrichs, a gay German author writing in the late nineteenth century, sought to understand his own same-sex desires in a culture with rigidly heteronormative ideas of sexuality and gender. Ulrichs's work addressed topics of love and sex between men at a time when the word "homosexual" was first coming into use. Ulrichs was attempting to understand why some men were attracted to men and some women to other women. Ultimately, he concluded that some men had an innate "womanness"—that their spirit or psyche (sometimes translated as "soul") was female and thus they were drawn to other men. He expressed this as "anima muliebris virili corpore inclusa," Latin for "a female spirit trapped within a male body." He also postulated that women were sexually attracted to other women because they had a male psyche.

When Dr. Harry Benjamin, an early pioneer in transgender medicine, began providing care to trans people in the 1950s, he worked from the "trapped in the wrong body" model. Benjamin presumed that trans individuals had an even more pronounced disparity than the one described by Ulrichs—a fully developed male brain in a female body or vice versa. This medicalization of trans people led to one conclusion: as the brain was inalterable, the only way to rectify the mismatch was to change the body.

Benjamin's 1966 *The Transsexual Phenomenon* gave birth to the Harry Benjamin International Gender Dysphoria Association (later WPATH, the World Professional Association for Transgender Health), an organization that developed the original Standards of Care for the evaluation and treatment of transgender people. The initial protocols established a rigid timeline that involved psychotherapy and a "real life" test, in which a person had to live as a member of their desired gender for a year or more prior to any medical interventions (e.g., someone transitioning from male to female living publicly as a woman without yet beginning hormones). Only after these was a person given access to hormones and, later, surgery.

The Standards of Care set forth a series of questions by which individuals were evaluated to determine if they were appropriate candidates for treatment. Did they demonstrate that they had any ability to live as the gender they were assigned at birth? Were they showing grief or regret about their decision to leave behind the gender they were assigned at birth or their natal genitalia, or were they displaying a connection to the stereotypical interests of their assigned gender? Did they express sexual interests that might result in non-heterosexual identity after transition? Answering yes to any of these was considered proof that a person did not have the body/brain incompatibility that made them validly trans.

Unfortunately, this also limited possible identities and ensured that traditional binary and heteronormative social roles were maintained: people were permitted to transition only because transitioning made them "normal."

Some in trans and gender-nonconforming communities were invested in the "trapped in the wrong body" narrative and considered it authentic to their experiences. They felt it provided them with a way to understand the agony and dysphoria they had struggled with for much of their lives.

Other trans people, less convinced by this theory, nevertheless tacitly accepted it in order to receive care. This created a cycle of cultural and medical reinforcement: trans people heard from other trans people that their care depended on this story, so they told it to professionals, who began to hear only this story, a narrative that became further entrenched until "trapped in the wrong body" developed into the only acceptable narrative of trans identity.

As this narrative took hold, so did unproven biological theories that reinforced it. The most popular of these is the idea that hormones in utero can affect the brain separately from the body. The idea is that, at a key point in development, the fetal brain undergoes a chemical bath that, under "normal" circumstances, differs for males and females. The brains of transgender people, proponents argue, are instead awash in chemicals appropriate for the "opposite" gender, and this is said to influence the developing brain to acquire structures more typical for the gender "opposite" that of their genetic makeup.

Because it would be unethical and risky to perform procedures to measure hormone levels in developing fetuses, prenatal hormone studies rely on "proxy markers," such as finger-length ratios, thought to correlate to hormone exposure, and compare these markers in transgender and cisgender people. To date, there is no conclusive evidence that proxy markers of hormone exposure correlate with transgender identity. To add to the confusion, and despite the lack of evidence, identical theories including hormonal exposure and proxy markers for this exposure have been simultaneously used to explain both homosexual and transgender identities, but we know that these are not the same.

Another avenue of research aimed at understanding the influence of intrauterine hormones is the investigation of gender identity in intersex people—formerly known by the outdated term "hermaphrodites"—those whose physical makeup does not neatly match either male or female. Intersex people may have chromosomes that vary slightly from XX or XY, or they may have genitalia that do not match norms. Intersex people have long been the subjects of research, often against their will, and many have spoken out against their identities being used as evidence for particular theories. There are many ways to be intersex, and gender identity differs depending on the intersex condition, but there may be increased rates of desire for change from a birth-assigned gender among certain groups of intersex people. Still, overall, intersex people are most likely to identify with the gender they are assigned at birth, regardless of what we know about their hormone exposure.

Finally, researchers have also turned to animal studies to better understand the influence of hormonal exposure on gender identity. Animals whose hormonal exposure is manipulated in utero have been shown to demonstrate behaviors that researchers categorize as more typical of the other gender, such as female rats attempting to mount other rats. However, the nature of these behaviors complicates the picture. Is sexual mounting (i.e., the position an animal takes in a secual encounter) a gendered behavior or a marker of some aspect of sexuality? Is a female rat that is exposed to "male" hormones and mounts other rats gay or transgender? What if she mounts male rats—is she heterosexual but domineering? Because we cannot ask animals about their inner thoughts and feelings, the utility of animal studies of gender identity and sexuality is limited.

In addition to research related to hormone exposure, genetics and brain anatomy have been targets of investigation. Transgender people, in general, have been shown to have the chromosomal makeup expected based on their gender assigned at birth. Scientists have also looked at particular genes that might be involved in transgender identity but have come up empty-handed.

Brain anatomy and physiology are popular areas of investigation today, both because they are in line with the "trapped in the wrong body" theory and because there has been limited funding for brain research. A few small studies have found differences in brain anatomy or functioning between transgender and cisgender people, but most have numerous flaws, including too few participants or confounding factors such as participants having taken hormones. There remain no conclusive studies linking transgender identity to brain structure or function. In addition, even those researchers with strong beliefs that the brains of transgender people are different from those of cisgender people argue that our current theories are not nuanced enough. According to the Spanish psychobiologist Antonio Guillamon, "Trans people have brains that are different from males and females, a unique kind of brain. It is simplistic to say that a female-to-male transgender person is a female trapped in a male body."

Many social scientists interested in gender and sexuality have written about the ways in which our society attempts to apply a rigid notion of biological differences between men and women in order to enforce the gender binary. Molecular biologist Anne Fausto-Sterling argues that the belief that men and women have distinct, clearly differentiated brains is a fallacy. In her books she examines the literature and science of gender, concluding that men's and women's brains are virtually identical and that even neuroscientists have difficulty identifying one from the other. Additionally, she reports that there is greater variability within the brains of one gender than between those of men and women. Similarly, sociomedical scientist Rebecca Jordan-Young, author of *Brain Storm: The Flaws in the Science of Sex Differences*, asserts that we are all too quick to accept faulty studies that rely on unproven assumptions because they fit our theories that men's and women's brains are inherently different.

It is likely that gender identity is influenced by both biological and social factors, and that these forces impact each other in ways that we may never understand. Nevertheless, the politics of "trapped in the wrong body" remain with us, and contending with them is complex.

While some in trans communities believe that transness is biological and the foundation of their true selves, others feel that they have come to their trans identity out of an ongoing exploration of gender and that their understandings of themselves have been influenced by culture and gender norms.

This is not merely an abstract debate. Arguing that transness is not a choice has afforded us rights, including legislation granting access to appropriate bathrooms, antidiscrimination statutes, and protections for trans youth in schools. Identity categories to which a person belongs by no fault of their own, such as race and sex, generally receive more public support when it comes to antidiscrimination laws. Trans advocates are actively working to compel insurance companies to reimburse treatment, including hormones, surgeries, and sometimes procedures such as electrolysis and vocal training, with the argument that transness is biological. If we argued that trans people had a "choice," insurance providers would likely categorize these interventions as cosmetic and not medically necessary. This would make transition financially unattainable for so many in our communities.

On the other hand, acquiescing to the idea that trans people have no say in their own identity, that they are driven entirely by their biology, strips them of their self-determination. The argument that being trans is not a choice also subtly gives power to the idea that being trans is a bad thing, something to be sought out in young children and eradicated in any way possible, something no one would choose if the choice was available.

"Trapped in the wrong body" remains a valid narrative for many people. But our community deserves more options.

Informed Consent philosophies of care, developed at LGBTQ+ health centers in the 1990s, do not rely on notions of a fixed medical narrative of being "broken" and seeking to be "fixed" but acknowledge the right of individuals to determine their own gender, whether their ultimate expression of gender matches cultural stereotypes or not. Informed Consent provides people more flexibility to understand their own identities in ways that seem comfortable for them and to make decisions about medical treatment as consenting adults, rather than by appealing to medical providers as judges. The modern WPATH Standards of Care have moved in this direction.

Some people think of transness as a natural human variation and see trans and gender-nonconforming people as representing the broad diversity of how human beings can express the gendered aspects of human identity. For them, it is not about being damaged but about being different. And many have set aside altogether the need to find a cause or justify our transitions through biology.

Today, many of us recognize that all people have the ultimate authority to decide about their gender. Gender is a part of human existence to be toyed with, explored, questioned, deconstructed, and lived in an infinite variety of expressions. We step outside social conventions of gender to wonder what gender might really *be* underneath the cultural constructions, what fundamental truths or novel understandings we might discover. We often defy easy classification.

For some, though maybe not for all, gender can be a choice. But any narrative of trans identity is valid.

Trans People Are Secretly Gay

You're walking down the street and suddenly hear someone shout "fag!" at another person. Picture in your head who you're expecting to be the target of this verbal assault. It could be an effeminate gay man or a "butch" lesbian, but it could just as easily be a trans woman. Why?

Gender identity—our internal sense of our own gender—and sexual orientation—the gender(s) of the people we are attracted to—are distinct concepts that are often conflated. Lesbians are frequently seen, in the popular imagination, as more masculine than most women, while gay men are often perceived as being more feminine than other men. Because of common confusion between gender identity and sexual orientation, trans people are sometimes assumed to be motivated to transition because of their sexual orientation. Those who identify as gay or lesbian after transition often get the question "What was the point of transitioning?" as if the ultimate goal of transition is to become straight.

Many people imagine gay and trans people existing on a spectrum. This confusion, in Western culture, dates back to the 1860s with the advent of early sexology. Thinkers and social progressives such as Karl-Maria Kertbeny and Karl Ulrichs introduced the idea of the "invert" or "urning" to explain homosexual desire. According to their theories, coincidentally developed separately but at the same time, people with sexual desires for someone of the same gender felt this way because they had the "soul"—their word for an essential inner quality—of the so-called opposite gender. Because heterosexuality was understood as "natural," same-sex desire *must* be caused by opposite being attracted to opposite. This makes little sense to us today and is easy to ridicule. But it is important to remember that these men were attempting—as a way to make life easier and safer for homosexuals—to move away from the idea that same-sex behavior was a sin and a crime, and were trying to postulate a "natural" explanation for it.

Today, the discussion centers on gender identity. We understand that sexual orientation is a completely different concept from gender identity. However, when parents or teachers discuss children who are exploring their identities, they often frame the conversation as a question of whether a child is trans or "just gay." Like the early sexologists, they are making unfounded and inaccurate assumptions due to a lack of understanding.

Gender identity and sexual orientation come in many different permutations. Transgender people can be gay, straight, bisexual, or pansexual, just like anyone else. Many trans people see their sexual orientation as unrelated to their gender identity—if they are attracted exclusively to one gender, for example, prior to transition, this will remain the same after transition. However, there are also trans people who say that transition has affected their attractions and desires. In a study of 452 transgender and gender-nonconforming people in Massachusetts published in 2016, 42.7 percent identified as queer, 15.7 percent as bisexual, 12.2 percent as straight, 10.4 percent as gay or lesbian, and 19.0 percent as other. Among those who transitioned, 64.6 percent reported a change in attractions post-transition. After transition, some people's sexual orientations may expand to include a larger group of people, while others' attractions may narrow. Many trans men, for example, identify as lesbians prior to transition, but afterward begin to realize attractions to men. Some believe that taking testosterone influences their sexuality, while others feel that their new role as men allows them to interact intimately with other men in more comfortable ways than they could when they presented as women.

Just as transgender people can have a wide variety of sexual orientations, gay and lesbian people can have an array of gender identities and expressions. Within lesbian communities, there are a range of gender presentations, from "lipstick lesbians" (extremely feminine) to "butches" (hardened appearing and masculine) and everything in between. Some lesbian relationships appear (to the outsider) to follow traditional butch/femme heterosexual roles, but many don't. Heterosexuals also vary widely in their gender presentation. Some straight women enjoy playing or watching sports, hunting, or wearing stereotypically masculine clothing. The word "metrosexual" was coined to describe straight men whose well-maintained appearance might give the impression of homosexuality.

Effeminate men are often ridiculed for their gendered behaviors. And, historically, "mannish" women were mocked for their demeanor and dress. Gay and lesbian people can be discriminated against because of their gender expressions and not necessarily for their sexual orientations. Some researchers in gender and sexuality studies believe that a significant portion of homophobia is predicated on discomfort with gender nonconformity rather than with differing sexuality. These scholars point to the increased bullying that gender-nonconforming children face—especially effeminate boys—compared to those who display more stereotypical gender roles. A 2012 article in the journal *Pediatrics* demonstrated that childhood gender nonconformity is a predictor of bullying, abuse, PTSD, and, later, depression and suicidality. Adult gay and lesbian people also face more stigma when they are gender nonconforming, even from within LGBTQ+ communities. Some gay men describe themselves as "straight-acting" when they use hook-up sites such as Grindr or OkCupid.

Since the advent of the LGBTQ+ movement, and because of political activism, gay and lesbian people have increasingly become more accepted in American society. More recently, transgender issues have moved into the spotlight, and some political gains have been attained. While there are many positive effects of these changes, there are also some troubling trends. Gays and lesbians who fit gender norms, by getting married and having children, are more welcomed into mainstream society. The same is true of transgender people who fit into the gender binary. Many individuals who do not blend in as seamlessly are left out. In many ways, this new "acceptance" only serves to further marginalize the people who are already the most marginalized.

The separation of gender identity from sexual orientation allows some gay and lesbian people to distance themselves, politically, from trans people. While most organizations today use the umbrella term "LGBT" to describe their membership, some gay people argue that LGB and T people have different needs and should therefore work separately so as to avoid outsiders viewing them as the same. These arguments illustrate the shame that many gay and lesbian people have about their own wide range of gender expression and their desire to divorce themselves from gender nonconformity.

Although gender and sexuality are not the same, they may be connected in ways that we do not yet understand. Research has shown that a greater percentage of gay and lesbian than straight people were gender nonconforming as children. What this means is unclear, and by no means are all gay or lesbian people gender nonconforming early in life. However, there is evidence that gender nonconformity is common in LGB communities. And, just as important, the oppression of LGB people is linked to their gender expression. This makes it important to build coalitions between LGB and T communities to fight gendered oppression together.

It's Rude to Ask How You Should Address Someone

What's in a name?

In many cultures, a name denotes a person's gender. We are conditioned from early in life to regard names as masculine or feminine depending on their history and their last letters. Most names are unambiguous and suggest a specific, binary gender, although gender-neutral names have become more popular recently.

Adopting a new name and new pronouns is a central part of transition. The move from birth name to preferred name is about altering both how we think of ourselves and how we expect others to view us; the new name is a reflection of who we were, who we are, and who we hope to become. The choice can be a positive affirmation and a statement to one's world that we, as individuals, have made the decision upon our own authority to pursue a different course for our existences than those anticipated by our family and society. It is an act of empowerment.

And after a lifetime of being referred to by signifiers we have considered inauthentic, new labels can be a liberation. In short, a lot is wrapped up in a name and pronoun.

Referring to people by their chosen name and pronoun is a basic demonstration of respect. How are others to know how to speak about someone in transition? There is a simple and obvious answer: ask. Politely. Trans people would generally prefer a respectful conversation about their correct name and pronoun than to have someone make a mistake based on an assumption or ignorance.

Transition can be jarring for outsiders, especially the adjustment to new names. Family, friends, and coworkers have known us by our birth names for years, sometimes decades. Our parents may have selected our birth names to honor a loved one who has passed or to reflect a sentiment important to them. Changing a name may give the impression that we are dismissing that legacy—that we are being hostile to our families or even to our cultural backgrounds. Our birth names and assigned genders are imprinted on their brains.

Many cisgender people—even allies—may have trouble using a person's new name or pronoun. When trans people are misgendered or called the wrong name, it can be difficult to tell if someone is being rude, habitual, or simply clueless. For trans and gender-nonconforming people, the experience can sometimes be severely upsetting.

Some allies will be fine immediately; others will take time to adjust. Trans people have radically altered how we want others to understand us, and early transition is such a painful experience that we often crave compassion and empathy; it can be difficult for us to have kindness toward others when we are suffering ourselves. All we may yearn for during this time is a hug and acknowledgment, but this may be precisely when our allies are most distant.

Parents or others may need time to grieve an individual's pre-transition gender and the name associated with it, both because that name and gender may have been coupled with particular wishes and aspirations, and also because birth names often have other meanings important to those around us. It requires patience to remember that our families are transitioning as well. An adjustment that happens gradually may not be a sign of disrespect.

Other times people do not recognize just how profound a name and pronoun can be. Many trans and gender-nonconforming people find our birth names so dissonant that we become triggered simply by hearing them uttered. Our pretransition lives so often demanded that we endure daily bullying, stigma, shame, anxiety, and depression, that existence became chronic trauma. Our birth names often recall each and every moment when we were harassed by classmates or sat alone in our bedrooms in misery, hopeless and despairing that we could ever manifest the people we knew ourselves inside to be, aware that our families or loved ones or employers or communities might never accept us, and terrified of the violence we might encounter within our homes or when we stepped outdoors. To hear ourselves called by the wrong name can be an uncomfortable reminder of an earlier life we struggle to put behind us.

Some trans and gender-nonconforming people use the term "deadname" to refer to their birth names, making unambiguous that they consider themselves reborn as new individuals and that their pretransition names and identities are no longer in existence. "Deadnaming"—calling someone by their birth name—is a profound insult when done deliberately and is often used as a means to ridicule and reject our trans identities. An example of this is when conservative commentators purposely refer to Caitlyn Jenner as "Bruce," a blatant dismissal of her as a woman and of trans people altogether. This is often extremely distressing to someone with a traumatic past or someone preferring to distance themselves from their pretransition identity.

Other trans people feel no such need to separate their current self from their past and consider their birth names to be signifiers of the people they once were and now have evolved beyond, much the way someone might have had a previous career or last name before marriage but no longer. These individuals judge it a historical truth that they once were that pretransition individual, with a different gender, name, and other attributes. And yet, though it may be less agonizing to such people, it remains just as inappropriate to call someone by a birth name or pronoun when that person has requested something else.

Many allies develop significant anxiety thinking about what a trans person would like to be called and wonder if they will inadvertently offend a person by asking about pronouns, whereas many trans people advise allies not to overthink it. In a 2014 speech at Haverford College in Pennsylvania, Laverne Cox told the students about a recent clinic visit during which a nurse had introduced himself by saying, "Hi, I'm David. My preferred pronouns are 'he' and 'him.' What about you?" Cox, despite presenting as clearly female, said that she wished more people would introduce themselves this way.

There is some discussion within trans communities about whether the word "preferred" should be used to describe a person's pronouns, as many trans people feel that their pronouns are simply reflective of who they are and are not what they "prefer." Instead of using the term "preferred gender pronoun," or PGP, some trans people suggest that allies ask "What pronouns do you use?" or "What are your pronouns?"

Recently, many colleges have started to introduce the practice of asking for pronouns into classes and other activities. This has garnered considerable backlash from conservative professors and students. In 2016, the University of Michigan began to allow students to add their preferred pronouns to its database through the university's website to inform professors of students' pronouns. A Fox News opinion piece titled "Student Single-Handedly Defeats an Army of Gender Neutral Activists" praised a conservative student who logged in and, "in order to point out how absurd this new policy is," gave himself the pronoun "His Majesty."

In September 2016, University of Toronto psychology professor Jordan Peterson posted a video on YouTube titled "Professor Against Political Correctness: Part 1," in which he spoke against a Canadian bill that would increase protections for gender identity and expression, and stated that he would refuse to use gender-neutral pronouns. More than 250 faculty members signed on to a letter in protest. Peterson, ignoring the presence of intersex and nonbinary people, later told a *VICE* reporter, "I don't know what the options are if you're not a man or a woman. . . . It's not obvious to me how you can be both because those are, by definition, binary categories."

Though many other professors have successfully integrated into their classrooms the practice of asking for gender pronouns, even some who are generally in support of transgender students have, at times, wondered about the potential drawbacks of having every student name their pronoun in a public setting. In a 2016 *New York Times* op-ed, Elizabeth Reis, a professor of gender studies at the City University of New York's Macaulay Honors College, wrote that "this ice-breaking ritual, in my experience, is easy only for those for whom the answer is obvious. It can 'out' or isolate others, particularly those who are still considering their gender or who have just begun to transition."

During one early class session, when Reis instructed the students to go around the room introducing themselves and giving their names and pronouns, one student who looked traditionally male gave a female name and pronouns. "This is the kind of student for whom we might think the pronoun exercise would be perfect," wrote Reis. "Once she identified herself, no one would accidentally mis-gender her in class. But in fact, as the student explained to me later, having to say her pronouns in a room full of strangers terrified her. She would have preferred to state her female name and leave it at that." After this experience, Reis tried a new strategy with her next class. She had students give their first names and add their pronouns if they desired. She wrote, "This strategy seemed to work. Half of the students disclosed their pronouns and the other half just introduced themselves in the standard way. No one became the object of scrutiny."

Once someone has asked about another person's pronouns, the next step is starting to use them. While switching from "he" to "she" (or vice versa) may be difficult for the network of allies and others surrounding binary transpeople, or around those who "pass," it can be more problematic when the individual identifies as gender nonconforming, genderqueer, or as some other variety of nonbinary gender. Binary people fit into traditional norms, and so even if someone is changing which pronouns they use, the pronouns themselves are familiar.

Nonbinary people who feel their genders do not align with traditional cultural norms may use a wide variety of pronouns, or sometimes even none at all. "He" or "she" does not capture their identities and often feels too simplistic to encompass the more nuanced and complex genders of those outside the binary.

"They"/"their" is common, and though some people find this awkward because it might seem to imply a plural, it has historically been used to denote a singular individual when the gender of the person being referred to is not clear. For example, a professor might ask, "Who left their notebook here last week?" or a doctor might say, "Each patient should bring in a copy of their results."

Genderfluid people whose sense of self fluctuates may even alter their preferred pronouns on a daily basis depending on their feelings or expressions on any given day, making it even more confusing to outsiders.

Other people use pronouns that are new or of their own invention, such as "xi"/"xir" and "ze"/"zir." Some use their own name or initial as their pronoun. For example, Justin Vivian Bond, a trans performance artist, prefers the straightforward "V."

Titles, like pronouns, can be male, female, or gender neutral. Most men use "Mr.," and women generally choose from among "Miss," "Mrs.," and "Ms." However, there are also a variety of gender neutral titles, such as "Mx." (pronouned "mix"), "Misc." (pronounced "misk"), and "Mre." (pronounced like the word "mystery").

Trans and gender-nonconforming people are addressing fundamental issues of our identities, our bodies, and how we relate to the world. Those who do their best to use our preferred names and pronouns allow us to feel respected and safe.

TIPS FOR TRANS PEOPLE

How to tell someone your correct name and pronoun

- "I'm not sure if you're aware, but I'm in the process of changing my gender. I just wanted you to know that I am now going by the name XYZ and prefer the pronoun PDQ."
- You do not have to answer any additional questions if you do not want to.

How to handle it when someone uses the wrong name or pronoun

- Stick up for yourself! And try educating them if you feel you can. While there is no need for more disclosure than is comfortable, you may be able to simply say, "I'm trans and go by the name X and prefer [male/female/neutral] pronouns."

TIPS FOR ALLIES

How to ask about someone's pronouns

- Step 1: Politely say: "Can I ask what pronouns you use?"
- Step 2: After the person answers, say, "Thank you."
- Step 3: Move on.

What to do if you call someone the wrong name or pronoun

- Step 1: Apologize.
- Step 2: Move on.
- Making it into an "issue" is often more uncomfortable for the trans person than a simple acknowledgment.

"Sure, I'd Love to Talk About What's in My Pants"

We all maintain a balance between public and private. Some aspects of our lives we freely share with others, while other facets we keep confidential, retain as personal, and hold close to ourselves.

What we have underneath our clothes usually falls into the second category.

And yet when talking to someone trans or gender nonconforming, many people seem intent on peeking up our skirts, inside our shirts, or down our pants. From the day we come out, we are assaulted by never-ending questions about our bodies:

"Are you having surgery?"

"When are you having surgery?"

"What was surgery like?"

"Do/does your new (chest/breasts/vagina/penis) look real?"

"Were you disgusted by your (chest/breasts/vagina/penis) before?"

"Can you actually have sex?"

"Can your sexual partners tell you're trans?"

"Can you orgasm???"

And countless others. Of course, the idea of posing similar questions to a random cisgender individual on an everyday city or rural street corner is an absurd thought. In short, this is an area where double standards clearly apply.

There has always been a fascination with trans bodies. Curiosity abounds. Gender is a fundamental way we categorize individuals, and when we encounter individuals who do not easily fit within the gender they were assigned at birth, there is a natural inquisitiveness, a desire to comprehend, and an intuitive need to talk. We may simultaneously shove the peculiar thing away, since "it" is other than "us," odd and dissimilar. Perverse. Frightening. Often unacceptable. The unusual can make us uncomfortable.

Trans people defy the typical "penis=male" and "vagina=female" associations of identity with genitals, and so those not in the trans community frequently feel compelled to ask personal questions, often without recognizing the impact their questions may have on the person being asked. Where they insist on probing are the very places we are most sensitive.

Through writing and media interviews, there are those trans and gender nonconforming people who happily spread ourselves bare for all to see. Such individuals believe that by divulging personal information we provide accurate education from a first-hand source. Doing so can be an act of claiming power over one's narrative, and proactively influencing what is said about us individually and as a group. This way, nontrans people get the real story, not one manufactured and spun for public consumption by others who may have political agendas.

In the groundbreaking 1996 book *Body Alchemy: Transsexual Portraits*, Loren Cameron and several of his transmasculine peers published explicit photography and writing about their transitions. Neophalluses, reconstructed chests, befores-and-afters . . . all were exposed in finely grained, black-and-white 8x10 glossies. Some images had accompanying text in which the genitals' owners described their joyful and anguished relationships with their bodies. For many people this would be mortifying, but for the book's participants, this was clearly liberating.

Western culture has a long history of objectifying and putting on display those it sees as different. For example, Saartjie Baartman, a woman born a slave in South Africa circa 1789 and sold to a circus showman, was exhibited throughout England and France as a carnival sideshow "exhibit," undressed or in a skintight bodysuit, for the captivation of the masses. She was *different*; she was a large woman and it is said she had a particularly significant bottom, breasts, and labia along with ebony skin still uncommonly seen in Europe. Taken together, these features only accentuated that she was utterly unlike the "dignified" Caucasian women of Europe. She was compared occasionally to an orangutan rather than to a woman. Baartman became known as the "Hottentot Venus," and she, or more accurately certain parts of her, *were* the exhibit.

A century and a half later, transgender people's naked bodies were being scrutinized in similar ways. Christine Jorgensen, one of the first publicly known trans women in the United States, had served in the US Army during World War II and was greeted upon her return from surgery in Denmark in 1952 with great fanfare. She was an instant celebrity the moment her fashionable pumps hit the tarmac, but she simultaneously became someone obsessively scrutinized. Were her shoes too big? Was her chest hairy? Could she actually have sex? Who would she have sex with?

This curiosity persists today, and is often forced upon us. Trans people are the current peep show on display to the masses, and usually it is our genitals that are the starring acts.

That said, some transgender and gender-nonconforming people recognize that disclosure is a choice; we have the authority to say "yes" or "no" or "I'd rather not answer" or "fuck off."

Some of us have been willing to exercise this right, rejecting the demands of others to enter our private lives. Christine Jorgensen herself stormed off a 1968 television interview with talk-show host Dick Cavett after being asked about her sex life.

And more recently, in 2014, on Katie Couric's daytime talk show, actress Laverne Cox and model Carmen Carrera repeatedly deflected questions about their bodies, Carrera saying, "I don't want to talk about it; it's really personal." At one point, Cox finally shut down the line of questioning for good, responding that there were far more critical topics to discuss:

> I do feel there is a preoccupation with [genitals]. The preoccupation with transition and surgery objectifies trans people. And then we don't get to really deal with the real lived experiences. The reality of trans people's lives is that so often we are targets of violence. We experience discrimination disproportionately to the rest of the community. Our unemployment rate is twice the national average; if you are a trans person of color, that rate is four times the national average. The homicide rate is highest among trans women. . . . By focusing on bodies, we don't focus on the lived realities of that oppression and that discrimination.

Invasive questions about transgender bodies imply that we can be classified according to what we have under our clothes. Being asked about topics generally off limits in polite conversation insinuates that we no longer have the right to privacy, that intimate details about our lives are open for discussion, even without our consent.

Asking about medical procedures before, during, or after an individual has transitioned would never be permissible in other areas of society. Genitals, and the decisions trans and gendernonconforming people make about them, are intensely personal. Genitals can be markers of trauma, pleasure, shame, embarrassment, delight, pride, anger, dysphoria, and other complex emotions that may or may not relate to someone's sense of identity.

Who we are is not reflected by what's between our legs. Surgery and other body modifications are one aspect of the trans "experience"—something people may or may not choose to undergo—but either way, decisions about surgery are intensely private and personal.

PART 2

SEX AND RELATIONSHIPS

MYTH 8

Most Trans People Are Sex Workers and Have HIV

Once relegated to the shadows, transgender and gender-nonconforming people are increasingly visible in movies, television, books, and other media. While depictions are gradually more positive than before, many still rely on the dated, stigmatizing tropes that most or all of us who are trans or gender nonconforming do sex work, or that all transgender people are HIV positive.

Unfortunately, it is true that rates of HIV and other sexually transmitted infections among trans people are exceptionally high. A National Institutes of Health report from 2009 documented that approximately one-third of all transgender people in the United States were HIV positive and that an overwhelming number had been unaware of their HIV status, positive or negative. Another study evaluated the rates of HIV in transgender women in New York City, finding that *nearly half* of the African American and Latina transgender women were HIV positive; this compares to just 3.5 percent of the Caucasian transgender female population. While trans men generally have lower rates of HIV infection (0–3 percent), those who sleep with cisgender men are at higher risk.

To put these elevated HIV rates in context, transgender people demonstrate a variety of health disparities compared to the general population and even compared to cisgender (nontransgender) members of lesbian, gay, bisexual, and queer communities. The rate of diabetes in transgender individuals is estimated at 25.9 percent compared to 13.7 percent in LGB individuals. Almost 40 percent of transgender and gender-nonconforming individuals are obese, compared to 24.6 percent of cisgender people. Smoking prevalence is 30.7 percent among transgender and gender-nonconforming populations versus 15.4 percent in the general population. And it has been found that up to *42.3 percent of transgender adults report a history of a suicide attempt.*

These statistics clearly document the ongoing public health crises in transgender and gender-nonconforming populations.

The numbers of transgender and gender-nonconforming people engaged in sex work are also high and show similar ethnic divisions to the transmission rates of HIV. Those identifying as black or black/multiracial are most likely to practice sex work (39.9 percent). In Hispanic/Latinx individuals the rates are nearly as high (33.2 percent), while in white individuals they are significantly lower (6.3 percent).

Why are these numbers so elevated?

Many transgender people have been marginalized from a young age. Children and adolescents who demonstrate gender variance can be harassed by their peers simply for dressing in the "wrong" garment or for having a hairstyle that more closely matches norms for the "other" gender. Teachers often refuse to acknowledge students' trans identities and insist on referring to individuals by their birth names and pronouns, something most transgender and gender-nonconforming people find to be an aching nullification of their identity. Very frequently, youth who do not conform are subject to ostracization, jeers, bullying, physical violence, and sexual assault. Many youth also face similarly unsupportive or hostile families.

These explicit and implicit attacks can become a chronic trauma individuals face daily. Lack of physical and emotional safety can lead to poor school performance, less access to higher education, fewer opportunities for stable and lucrative employment, and less safe living conditions.

Transgender people can also face discrimination in hiring due to their appearance, gaps in resumes due to the time spent in transition and possibly out of the workforce, difficulty using past employers as references, and potentially mismatching identity documents. The 2011 National Transgender Discrimination Survey found that transgender people are four times more likely than others to have a household income of less than $10,000 per year and are twice as likely to be unemployed. For black transgender people, the unemployment rate is four times the national average.

Many in our communities are so uncomfortable with their bodies that they take inadequate care of their general health. They may not seek or have access to regular health care, especially pretransition, and may lack sufficient food or shelter. Additionally, 26.3 percent report misusing drugs or alcohol to cope with transgender-related discrimination.

Not surprisingly, all this leaves transgender and gender-nonconforming people especially vulnerable to poorer health, riskier lives, and fewer professional opportunities beyond marginalized careers like sex work.

Sex work comes in countless forms, any of which can be done by people trans or cis. Though sex work is a last resort for many, it is not always done in desperation. Transgender sex workers have consistently been in high demand and often find this type of work lucrative. Transfeminine people engage in sex work at nearly twice the rate of transmasculine people. Transgender pornography—primarily transgender women with functioning penises, but also transgender men with vaginas—is among the most sought-after forms of pornography. The largest consumer demographic for transgender porn is heterosexual men.

Less common today are stereotypical miniskirt-clad, stiletto-heeled women or musclebound, shirtless men alongside avenues beckoning to passersby. Those streetwalkers who do exist are often transgender adolescents rejected by their families with no other means to raise money. Their youth and powerlessness make them especially vulnerable and among the most defenseless in our communities.

Sex work is increasingly negotiated via computer or cell phone. Sex workers list themselves online in subsections of Craigslist or on sites devoted to an individual worker or agency. Here, potential clients are free to explore body types, areas of expertise, likes, dislikes, and boundaries at their leisure.

Sex work may not involve direct exchanges of bodily contact for cash. Instead it might include acting in pornographic movies, having photos taken, or online "camming," in which an individual performs as dictated by paying subscribers via webcam. Camming and online porn reach a wealthy and sometimes lonely demographic, often furtively watching at a safe distance from home or office, and well-designed cam websites facilitate the easy transfer of money from viewer to entertainer. Neither camming nor pornography involves actual human contact, and both provide a measure of safety for the sex worker.

Transgender people also function as escorts and "kept women." These individuals are often quite elegant, accompanying their clients to professional or cultural events; they may have brief or long-term relationships with clients. Some clients provide apartments and a monthly cash "allowance," essentially hiring these women as private mistresses available on demand.

Some transgender people turn to sex work when their financial situation becomes dire. "Survival sex" refers to an exchange of sex for basic needs: someone homeless might trade sex for a bed, or a substance addict might swap sex for drugs when unable to pay for another fix. Sex might be bartered for food, a rent payment, or as protection from violence. Similarly, transgender women in prison have historically been housed alongside cisgender male populations and may negotiate sex for food, privileges, or security.

Many in trans communities turn to sex work to raise the large sums of money necessary to transition. Though hormones may be covered by insurance companies, other necessary medical procedures, like hair removal and surgeries, generally are not. Many trans or gender-nonconforming people do not have health insurance at all.

Is the connection between sex work and HIV automatic? It generally depends on the level of risk people take when they engage in sex acts. Some sex workers have the ability to decide to use protection, or to say yes or no to proposals. Sex workers with the least power are essentially coerced because of desperation to agree to riskier sexual activities. Individuals performing survival sex, often those in marginalized communities due to race or socioeconomics and people who are incarcerated face additional pressures to engage in whatever the client demands.

The belief that sex work is inherently humiliating is not universal. Many trans and cisgender people involved in the industry report it to be a rewarding profession. Rather than finding the work demeaning or objectifying, many trans and cisgender people regard it as uplifting and sometimes approach the work believing they are providing moments of joy to lonely individuals who otherwise have few options for sexual or physical intimacy. Not everyone has the luxury of a partner. Some sex workers consider their trade akin to psychotherapy.

Sex workers who report a sense of empowerment also claim that this work provides body autonomy and sexual confidence. They feel desired and confident about their lives and bodies, and can raise large sums in short periods—money often needed for college or other expenses—leaving them free to pursue other activities without the drudgery of more time-consuming jobs. Many sex workers point out that our society has little difficulty with people who use their physicality for money in other ways (construction workers, dancers, athletes), and they feel that sex work is no different; they outright reject that sex work is morally wrong.

Organizations such as the Red Umbrella Project, the Sex Workers' Project, and the Sex Workers' Rights Advocacy Network center the experiences of sex workers and call for decriminalization of sex work and for additional services to aid sex-worker health and safety.

While the majority of trans people are neither sex workers nor HIV positive, there are higher rates of both in trans communities, especially among trans women of color. HIV rates correlate with marginalization, as do rates of sex work, although sex work is not always a sign of desperation. For some, it is even empowering.

Trans People Hate Their Bodies

Those of us who are trans and gender nonconforming have complicated relationships with our bodies. People frequently assume that we detest them—that we view ourselves in mirrors with disgust, loathe our genitals or chests, and regard our physical "shells" as foreign bits of flesh we can never accept.

The idea that we might happily use these parts for sexual pleasure is often shocking. To the physicians who first began working with trans people, those who enjoyed their genitals were seen as poor candidates for transition. Arousal signified that a positive relationship with our bodies was possible, and the recommended treatment was to deny access to hormones and surgery, and to encourage people to live as their assigned genders.

Though some trans people do have extreme dysphoria and an inability to experience sexual pleasure pre-transition, this certainly does not apply to everyone.

The idea of using our genitals for pleasure can be distressing for people who live in a body that feels inauthentic. Some trans people are unable to reconcile a coherent identity as their chosen gender while living in a body that does not match. They may "cut off" their genitals in their minds long before they have any surgeries. For some, the idea of using their genitals or other gender-related body parts for sexual enjoyment may trigger extreme revulsion. As a result, many trans people feel they cannot be sexually fulfilled until after surgery.

Many trans people who have difficulty integrating the reality of their bodies with how they see themselves may not just avoid sex but also take poor care of their bodies in general. They may not exercise or may overeat. They may not pay close attention to their bodies' rhythms and needs or may abuse alcohol or drugs. They may also feel extreme discomfort with seeking medical care, not wanting to think about, much less talk about and have examined, parts of their bodies that they do not identify with. A 2014 study at Fenway Health in Boston, published in the *American Journal of Preventive Medicine*, showed that transgender men were less likely than cisgender women to engage in routine pap testing to detect cervical cancer. In addition to reluctance to engage in health care because of body-image issues, trans people also fear they will receive poor care or be unable to find providers who respect their identities and are knowledgeable about transgender health. According to a 2015 study examining legal protections in public accommodations in Massachusetts, 24 percent of transgender people reported discrimination in health-care settings over the past year. Health-care discrimination was associated with worse mental and physical health, as well as increased instances of postponement of needed care.

Even if the genitals we were born with do not match the idealized images we have in our heads, dysphoria does not always mean we do not want to use what we have. Being sexual despite body issues is one way of doing this, but there are others. Some trans women use their sperm to produce biological offspring, for example, despite the widespread conception that the person who has contributed sperm is the "father."

Trans men also sometimes harvest their eggs to implant in a partner or surrogate, or become pregnant and give birth themselves. A 2014 web-based survey of forty-one transgender men who had been pregnant and delivered demonstrated that many had physically transitioned with testosterone prior to becoming pregnant. Of those on testosterone, 80 percent resumed voluntary menstruation within six months after stopping it. Almost half (46 percent) had undergone top surgery prior to conceiving. Participants discussed a number of issues that emerged for them as they planned for and then carried out their pregnancies. Some chose to see their experiences in gender-neutral or male ways, making statements like "My body was a workshop, building up this little kid" and "Pregnancy and childbirth were very male experiences for me. When I birthed my children, I was born into fatherhood." Others had a more difficult time with the dissonance of taking on such a traditionally female task: "Heavy time, having a baby, not passing as male, all the changes and a society telling me to just be happy."

For many trans people, the language they and others use to describe their bodies is important, and creativity can be key. Traditional words for genitalia can induce trauma; some trans people "relabel" their body parts to associate them with self-identified genders.

"Trannyclit" and "girlcock'"are occasionally used by transfeminine people and their partners when referring to what is commonly called a penis. Such words allow trans women to visualize their sexual organs—body parts they may or may not like but which they still retain and want to use. Trans men sometimes call their clitoris (which is often enlarged due to testosterone) a "dicklet" or their vagina a "manhole," "front hole," or "cockpit," and what we commonly call "breasts" they may rename simply their "chest." Applying male terms to structures traditionally thought of as female helps reconcile a body that does not conform to one's internal self-image, as does applying female terms for traditionally male biological organs.

Many in our community seek alternate ways to sexualize their bodies. It is not uncommon for transgender and gender-nonconforming people to engage in BDSM. An acronym combining the other acronyms B&D (bondage and domination), D&S (dominance and submission), and S&M (sadomasochism), the term refers to a subculture or activities that may involve role-playing, power dynamics, or the infliction or reception of pain as a form of pleasure. BDSM provides many benefits for trans people, often allowing for pleasure while also addressing our nontraditional relationships with our bodies.

BDSM is founded on open communication, and those involved discuss sexuality with frankness. Before engaging in contact, participants tell each other how they do or do not want to be touched and where. This open communication continues throughout the "scene." Anyone involved is able to stop the exchange at any point. BDSM provides structured environments in which people can speak openly about and meet their desires without fear of shame or retraumatization.

BDSM often involves forms of interaction that are not genital-centric. Many BDSM practices, such as spanking and flogging, focus on the back or buttocks. Bondage can provide an exhilaration that comes from controlled powerlessness. Role-playing allows the participants to creatively adopt other identities for limited times. Nontraditional bodies are not stigmatized but are appreciated or constructively fetishized, a direct opposite to the rejection and shame trans people often experience in mainstream settings.

In addition to the myth that few trans people enjoy their bodies prior to transition, there is a misconception that transgender people, especially transgender women, have little genital sensation after surgery and are unable to orgasm. However, a study of trans people post–genital surgery in England in 2006 found that all the trans men and 85 percent of the trans women were able to orgasm. A 2009 review echoed the high rates of orgasm after genital surgery. If you could before, you nearly always can after.

More and more trans and gender-nonconforming people are pursuing sexual liberation, rejecting society's expectations that we cannot love our bodies or take pleasure from them.

In a 2016 article, "How Trans Women Are Reclaiming Their Orgasms," Kai Cheng Thom relates how she was told by her doctor,

"'Most transsexuals find . . . their masculine sexual . . . *urges* are very disturbing to them. So that when they become women, they don't need orgasms.'" She felt despondent.

Thom continued,

> It wasn't until after I went home, feeling humiliated and crushed, that I really began to think about the implication of what [the doctor had] said: *When they become women, they don't need orgasms.* What the hell did that mean? That I had to choose between my sexuality and my gender identity as a woman? That trans women aren't supposed to have a sexuality?

Thom and countless others reject the notion that our orgasms are unimportant or secondary to our gender identity. We are reclaiming our sexualities and our abilities to structure and use our bodies as we choose, regardless of outdated myths or binary social norms.

Trans and gender-nonconforming people have the right and the ability to enjoy their sexualities. Furthermore, they have the right to be complete individuals engaged in the full range of the human experience.

MYTH 10

Trans People Are Trying to Trick Others

The 1992 film *The Crying Game* is arguably the most notable movie with a significant trans role. In it, the main character, Fergus, an Irish Republican Army operative, pursues a woman, Dil, whom he knows little about except that she is the former girlfriend of a man he captured. Like many other films and TV shows about trans people by nontrans people, including *Ace Ventura: Pet Detective, Crocodile Dundee*, and *The 40-Year-Old Virgin*, the "big reveal" is the trans character's trans identity. In *The Crying Game*, this reveal, to both the main character and the audience, comes as Dil undresses and we see her penis and scrotum. In predictable fashion, Fergus responds by running to the bathroom to throw up.

Trans people, especially trans women, are repeatedly cast as deceptive. A constant barrage of news stories portrays "unsuspecting" men who have been "fooled" into sleeping with trans women. Online forums such as Debate.org discuss whether it should be illegal for a trans person to sleep with someone without disclosing their trans identity. In 2013, a UK court of appeals sided with a teenage girl who claimed she had been sexually assaulted by a teenage trans boy because the two had dated and he had given her consensual oral and digital sex without disclosing that he was trans.

Though cisgender men are often painted as the victims in these stories, statistics demonstrate that it is the trans people who are commonly the subjects of emotional and physical violence. In August 2013, James Dixon and a few of his friends began chatting up a group of women on a New York City sidewalk. Among the women was Islan Nettles. Dixon reportedly asked Nettles if she was trans, and when she answered affirmatively, he began to beat her. He punched her so hard that her head hit the ground, causing her such serious brain injury that she died in a hospital five days later. "I just didn't want to be fooled," Dixon admitted during a police interview.

Every third day, a transgender person is reported murdered, and this is likely an underestimate, as many murders of trans people are never brought to the attention of authorities. Heterosexual cisgender men are, by far, the majority of perpetrators in these crimes, and there is social acceptability in some circles to claim "trans panic" as a defense—the idea that learning someone is trans can cause a temporary inability to prevent yourself from killing them. In 2014, California became the first state to ban "gay panic" or "trans panic" as defenses in court, but elsewhere in the United States these arguments are still permitted.

The concept of disclosure is very complex to a trans or gender-nonconforming person:

The first step in coming out is coming out to yourself. This can take a significant period of time—often years and sometimes decades. People who are exploring their gender identities often start by reaching out to online or in-person support groups in order to build community and hear stories so they can compare them to their own. Once they feel they understand themselves, they may begin to consider if and how to tell others.

Some trans people make a decision to be "stealth," keeping their identities private from all or most people. On the other end of the spectrum, there are those who feel it is important to be open to a large number of people about their identities, sometimes for political reasons. Almost all trans people are open to some people and not to others, and most fall somewhere in between these two ends of the spectrum.

Although there is often a lot of focus on trans people coming out to potential sexual or romantic partners, most people come out to those they are not intimately involved with, such as family, friends, and coworkers. Deciding who, how, and when to tell can be extremely complicated. For some people, coming out may not be a choice. For those who decide to make physical changes, it may be obvious to those around them that something is different about them.

For those who are able to make choices about coming out, there are many potential issues to consider: Who should you tell first? Will certain people feel hurt if they aren't the first to hear? Is the best way to come out in person or in a letter? Is there any possibility of physical danger in coming out?

Friends are different from family. Close friends are different from acquaintances. And strangers are something distinct altogether. Coming out at work may be unavoidable if you are changing gender markers on official paperwork, such as a Social Security card. For some people, it is possible to collaborate with their human resources department to maintain privacy from the rest of a company, but in small offices this may not be an option. Coming out to every stranger on the street is inappropriate and potentially dangerous.

Being transgender is not the only thing about ourselves that we disclose in different ways to different people. There are many other personal matters, such as health issues, whether we have children, and histories of incarceration, that we may keep private until we feel ready to share.

It can be especially challenging to decide if and how to disclose your trans status to a child or teenager. Children are at different developmental stages and may not see gender in the same ways as adults. For example, most small children have not yet learned that gender is usually stable, and they may believe that growing one's hair long or wearing certain clothes "magically" changes a person's gender. Adolescents may react with embarrassment or anger, or they may feel uncomfortable and take out their feelings on the person who is coming out. On the other hand, given the increasing openness to gender and sexuality issues among adolescents, teens may be some of trans people's greatest advocates.

One's stage in life and geography may affect how and when a person comes out. Young people starting college may have the privilege of leaving their high school and starting "fresh" in a new place—although, in the age of social media, it may no longer be possible to start over completely. People living in small towns may be forced to transition in a very visible way, often not by choice. Rural areas can be difficult places to come out but can also sometimes be surprisingly supportive.

For those trans people in intimate relationships, or hoping to find them, the decision whether and when to disclose can be one of the toughest. Many people, such as well-known author and *New York Times* columnist Jennifer Finney Boylan, are already in long-term relationships when they come to understand their trans identity. Some partners are aware that there is something "different" early on and may find the trans person's gendered feelings and behaviors attractive. For other partners, learning about someone's trans identity can be difficult, and some relationships end after disclosure. It can be one of the hardest choices of a trans person's life to decide to disclose if it means risking losing a long-term partner.

For trans people who are dating, every step of the relationship-building process with new potential partners can be anxiety provoking. For many, it feels like a catch-22: disclosing too early may not give someone enough time to get to know you as a whole person, while waiting too long can sometimes lead to feelings of betrayal. But when is too early and when is too late? Is it always important for trans people to disclose if they are interested in short-term sexual partners? What about in potentially unsafe situations? Trans people do their best to navigate these situations, and all people have the right to decide what will make them most comfortable. Everyone has different answers.

Often, when a heterosexual cisgender man is angry about a transgender woman not disclosing her history, it is because the man fears what it would mean to admit that he was attracted to her. Because the man fears social judgment from his peers and the implication that he might be gay, and because transgender people's identities are often not honored, cisgender men can suffer shame and ridicule for the possibility that they could be attracted to someone who currently has or ever had a penis. It only remains an attack on someone's masculinity to be attracted to someone with a penis if being gay is stigmatized. Were homophobia not so prevalent, a man who was initially attracted to a trans woman, but was no longer interested once he found out what body parts she had, could politely say so and move on without any stigma.

Popular media may focus on cisgender people who are "tricked" into believing a trans person is cis, but many trans people spend significant amounts of mental energy on managing disclosure, carefully working to keep themselves safe and maintain a basic level of privacy. Trans people make decisions on a daily basis about revealing information to friends, family, coworkers, acquaintances, and potential partners. Rather than painting them as deceptive, we should consider how difficult it is to face every day with such difficult questions about how to be who you are in the world.

MYTH 11

Most Trans People Can't Find Partners and End Up Lonely

Like so many others, the majority of transgender and gender-nonconforming people search for romantic and sexual partners with whom to share feelings and experiences; they also seek to give and receive comfort and to build a life with rich emotional and physical intimacy.

But there is a persistent myth that most trans people end up depressed and lonely. This belief is predicated on the notion that trans people are so maladjusted or outside the "norm" that they cannot be loved, and the assumption that there is something shameful about being attracted to trans people. There is also the underlying fear that being in a relationship with a trans person will make an otherwise heterosexual person gay. Though trans people do have dating and relationship challenges like everyone else, many enjoy thriving personal lives.

Sadly, the myth that trans people cannot find partners has a basis in truth. Trans and gender-nonconforming people often lament "dating while trans," finding it to be a disheartening experience. After claiming our true selves, or examining the meaning of gender in our lives, being unable to find a partner can instill loneliness and trigger depression. "Stigma by association," the stigma felt by those whose identities might be mainstream but who are around stigmatized people, or judgment from families or peers, can also be difficult for our potential partners.

Trans people often face rejection, including from those who might otherwise be interested. Jazz Jennings, a well-known trans youth activist, notes:

> Let's face it, your average straight cis-gender teenage boy isn't going to pursue a relationship with a trans-girl [sic]. Even if he does find her attractive, it could be social suicide if he acts on his feelings. I know this, because this is my life. . . . Boys flirt and hug my friends, but they just whisk by me as if I don't exist. Maybe they're afraid they'll get cooties, but this is high school so I doubt it's that—but it sure feels that way.

Jazz's situation is not uncommon. In a study of 889 trans people living in the United Kingdom, 79 percent agreed with the statement "When I think about having sex, I worry that there are very few people who would want to have sex with me." Some participants— experiencing their own dysphoria and their fear that others would not find them attractive—believed an active sex or romantic life was impossible until after surgical intervention. One study participant stated, "I used to fit into a neat category but now I don't, so it is hard to find sexual partners who are interested in me as I don't have what they are looking for."

Trans and gender-nonconforming people often develop social anxiety earlier in life due to internalized shame and fear of discrimination, which can hamper their dating even post-transition. Geography and age often also present problems. Younger people who live in urban or progressive communities have greater access to potential partners, but older people or those who live in conservative regions may face more difficulty.

Sometimes it is assumed that LGBQ+ people will be more open to dating trans partners than heterosexual people are, but the same biases often exist within queer communities. According to a recent survey by the dating site Match.com, less than half of LGBTQ+ people expressed openness to dating someone transgender or gender nonconforming.

Genderqueer people face specific obstacles. Not fitting into traditional male or female categories can make it difficult for others to classify them. People who are unfamiliar with genderqueer identities may not feel comfortable interacting with them or negotiating sex that does not necessarily have predictable roles.

Cisgender lovers of trans and gender-nonconforming people also face prejudice. "Stigma by association" was first described by Erving Goffman in 1963 as "courtesy stigma," and it refers to the process by which the people around an individual with a stigmatized identity are often subject to similar shame, abuse, and discrimination.

Dating someone trans can be challenging in other ways. A trans partner may or may not have the genitalia one is accustomed to. Many cis people report fear of not knowing how to make love to someone trans.

Identity issues are also complex. A cis man dating a trans woman—whether or not she has a penis—may wonder what this means for his sexuality or may fear that the relationship could make him appear to others as gay. In same-sex relationships, the opposite might be true. Some people consider sexuality to be about anatomy; for instance, a lesbian dating a trans woman may question her own sexuality or be afraid that others will interpret her as suddenly heterosexual, especially if the trans partner retains a penis, just as some gay men may wonder about their identity after having sex with someone who possesses a vulva.

In lesbian communities, identity issues often come up when one formerly female-identified partner transitions to male. "Lesbian" is, for some women, a political identity as much as a sexual one.

It can signify an opposition to a mainstream culture that has been oppressive to women. When one member of a couple transitions to male, the couple may begin to be perceived as straight. Cisgender lesbian partners of trans men often report feeling robbed of their countercultural sense of self when their partners transition.

But there is room for optimism. The UK trans study mentioned above documented significant improvement in confidence and empowerment with transition. "Being able to express this part of my identity sexually has definitely improved my sex life," said one respondent. Another commented, "Now I don't feel that my body is gross and icky; I can actually enjoy it!" The increase in comfort and connection to their bodies translated into a better sex life for these trans people.

Some study participants also reported that hormones improved their libido, and mental health: "Before transitioning my sex drive had become almost non-existent due to my depression," said one person. "Now that I have started transitioning I have become sexually active again."

Magazines and mainstream websites have begun catering to the increasing number of cisgender people dating trans people. Articles such as *Perks Magazine*'s "A Beginner's Guide to Dating a Transgendered Person," *Cosmopolitan*'s "12 Things You Should Know Before Dating a Transgender Guy," and *Everyday Feminism*'s "6 Things Every Man Who Dates Trans Women Needs to Know" address cis people's questions and concerns, and have made cis-trans relationships increasingly acceptable within the broader society.

Many trans people find success by dating within queer circles, which can be particularly fruitful environments for gender-nonconforming people and those still in mid-transition. Queer communities often view body norms as outdated. Traditional "penis-in-vagina" sex sometimes happens, though it may say nothing about the identities of the individuals involved. The broad mix of activities and identities within queer communities often leads to interactions that sexualize other areas of the body. Often, participants are focused more on mutual pleasure then on specific genitalia. Sex organs may or may not be associated with any particular gender. Sometimes body parts are simply body parts.

Ultimately, trans and gender-nonconforming people are happily engaged in relationships of all varieties, some living more straight-forward and heteronormative lives that include marriage and chil-dren, and others living radical, polyamorous, kinky lifestyles.

Whatever our bodies, identities, expressions, or orientations, we have an equal right to loving partners and rewarding romantic lives, and we are increasingly finding partners with whom to share these experiences.

Trans People Are a Danger to Others, Especially Children

Beliefs circulate through American culture that trans people are a risk to others—children, adolescents, women, and even sometimes adult men—usually due to misconceptions about trans people as sexual predators.

Even those who do not view trans people as sexually exploitative often insist that public visibility of those with non-heteronormative genders and sexualities encourages others to enter nontraditional lifestyles.

Whether as predatory vampires or harmful role models, transgender people have been demonized as threats, and many people believe that greater acceptance provides us greater opportunity to infect others. They would have us return to the closets, removed from public view, marginalized and out of contact with the general population. Often afraid of change, or rejecting that which they do not understand, they spread myths to discredit our identities and diminish our visibility.

There have been numerous attempts to legislate trans people's restroom use (see Myth 13, "'You're in the Wrong Bathroom!'") based on allegations that we are sexually exploitative. These laws are framed not as infringements on the rights of transgender people but as "protection" for women, children, and others. Those in favor of "bathroom bills" argue that trans people are more likely than others to perpetrate physical or sexual violence, or to spy on their neighbors while using the restroom. There is little discussion of the burden imposed on transgender and gender-nonconforming people when they are forced to use bathrooms inconsistent with their genders.

In fact, as of 2015, there had been no recorded incidents of anyone trans or gender nonconforming being arrested for sexual misconduct in a bathroom within the United States *ever*, and trans people are *far* more likely to be the victim in such settings. Up to 70% of transgender people report having been denied access to restrooms, harassed while using restrooms, or even physically assaulted.

Bathroom laws are perhaps the most publicized instances of transgender discrimination, but beliefs about trans people as sexual predators also lead to many other types of bigotry. When she transitioned in 2011, Marla Krolikowski, a high school teacher who had worked at the same school in Queens, New York, for thirty-two years, was fired. She reported being told by school officials she was "worse than gay." In a student-led movement, nearly six thousand people signed a petition in support of her reinstatement. In 2008, a trans man named Jan Buterman was fired from the Catholic school in Edmonton, Canada, where he taught. Though Canadian law supports the rights of transgender people, the school district spent over $367,000 in taxpayer dollars over the period from 2008 to 2016 to fight Buterman in court.

Transgender people have not only traditionally been suspect when working in schools but also in their own homes with their own children. There have been numerous cases of transgender people losing custody or visitation rights simply for being trans. In a well-known 1982 case, an Ohio court terminated visitation rights for a trans woman named Joni Christian when she transitioned. The psychiatrist called to testify felt that Christian's status as a transgender person would have a "sociopathic effect" on her children. The court stated that Christian "presented no evidence that [s]he was compelled by some mental imbalance to opt for a change in [her] sex" and asked, "Was [her] sex change simply an indulgence of some fantasy?" concluding that "the two minor children are in harm's way." In 2007, a Washington State court granted custody to the other parent when a transgender woman named Robbie Magnuson admitted that she was going to be having gender-affirming surgery. According to the court, "[Her] surgery may be everything [she] has hoped for, or it may be disastrous. No one knows what is ahead[,] and [t]he impact of gender reassignment surgery on the children is unknown." Also in 2007, in Nevada, a trans woman named Suzanne Daly lost her parental rights when she transitioned. The court blamed her, stating that "Suzanne, in a very real sense, has terminated her own parental rights as a father."

Transgender people are often treated similarly harshly in adoption cases. Only a handful of states have policies protecting against discrimination in adoption or fostering based on gender identity, allowing adoption agencies in most states to discriminate as they wish. Prior to the Supreme Court decision legalizing same-sex marriage, a number of transgender people had their adoptions challenged when the other parent claimed that the marriage was invalid. In 2004, a trans man named Michael Kantaras who was living in Florida formally adopted his child after his wife gave birth. When the couple divorced, Kantaras's wife argued that their marriage was invalid because it had been a "same-sex" marriage and that the adoption was void because Florida had a ban on adoption by gay people. The court stated that gender was "determined at birth" and that the marriage was therefore not valid; Kantaras was, for a while, stripped of his parental rights. Facing further appeals, the couple independently settled in 2005 for joint custody.

The decisions in these cases often contradict significant evidence that transgender people can make wonderful, loving parents. According to a review of research on transgender parents published by the Williams Institute in 2014, between one-quarter and one-half of transgender people report parenting children. Studies of youth with transgender parents have shown no differences in developmental milestones compared to children of cisgender parents. And while some people have concerns about the impact of having a transgender parent on children's gender identity and sexual orientation, studies have shown that parents' gender identity does not affect their child's gender identity or sexual orientation.

Some cities are beginning to recognize the positive impact that out LGBTQ+ people can have on youth. In 2013, New York City started an ad campaign to recruit LGBTQ+ people as foster parents. One billboard showed an interracial gay couple with a young girl and the caption read "Be the reason she has hope."

Despite fears, the reality is that the visibility of transgender and gender-nonconforming people, along with cultural acceptance of transgender individuals, has aided the mental and emotional health of some of our most vulnerable young people.

Fear of discrimination due to sexual orientation or gender identity can lead to depression, post-traumatic stress disorder, thoughts of suicide, and substance abuse. In a study based on data from the National Transgender Discrimination Survey, 42.3 percent of respondents reported having attempted suicide, and 26.3 percent reported misusing drugs or alcohol to cope with transgender-related discrimination. Family rejection was associated with increased odds of both behaviors, and the odds of engaging in such behaviors increased significantly with increasing levels of family rejection.

Many advocacy organizations have cited a lack of role models and cultural acceptance as contributing to isolation and depression, something even more problematic among communities of color.

In a 2015 *Marie Claire* article, activist and writer Janet Mock wrote that the cultural acceptance of multiple genders in her native Hawaii "served as a backdrop for my best friend and me as we embodied our womanhood, enabling us to transition through the halls of our high school and become who we knew ourselves to be." A 2016 study in the journal *Pediatrics* demonstrated that transgender children with supportive families have no more anxiety or depression than children who don't identify as trans.

Rather than being threatening to others, the visibility of trans and gender-nonconforming people contributes to the well-being of youth, both trans and cis, and to a safer, more civil society. Exposure to trans and gender-nonconforming individuals benefits our society both directly and indirectly. Normalizing transgender and gender-nonconforming lives through visibility on television, in movies, and in daily life offers role models people can identify with, especially during the agonizing process of coming out. Additionally, these representations help our allies address their own fears by seeing us in everyday settings, and they help everyone, trans or cis, explore the rich diversity of gender and sexuality by offering a vision of a broad range of possibilities for how we might live our lives.

PART 3

HEALTH AND SAFETY

MYTH 13

"You're in the Wrong Bathroom!"

You've been driving for eight hours straight. Two or three hours ago you stopped briefly to grab a cup of coffee and some gas, but it was already dark and the station attendant was staring just a little too long. You pushed on, and now you're getting desperate, even looking around your car, wondering if there's an old jar you could pee in if you pulled over. But what if a police officer saw you and decided to slow down? Would they think you were exposing yourself? Then you see a sign up ahead—rest stop five miles.

You have that far to consider the possibilities. You're wearing tight jeans and a blouse, hair to your shoulders, makeup. But you know you're recognizable as trans. Maybe there's a single-stall bathroom. If it's occupied and you have to wait, you might run into someone who doesn't like how you look. Especially now, in the middle of the night. A friend of yours was beaten up in broad daylight. You can't imagine what might happen to you at two in the morning at a highway rest stop. Should you call your sister to let her know you just crossed the state line . . . and that she should call you back in fifteen minutes? Is that crazy?

What if there is no single-stall bathroom? You can't go in the men's room the way you're dressed. You could be raped. And you're not a man. But if you go in the women's room, people there may glare at you or make rude comments. You heard about a trans woman who thought she was just being glared at, but when she walked out of the bathroom, someone's boyfriend or husband was there to knock her teeth out and drag her across the cement. Are you overthinking this? You put on your blinker and ease into the parking lot. There's a guy with his foot up on a car drinking a beer.

Transgender people have faced scrutiny and harassment in bathrooms for decades, but only recently has this discrimination become law. In 2013, Arizona was the first state to sponsor a "bathroom bill," which made it a crime to use a bathroom that did not correspond with your birth certificate. Fortunately, as the Transgender Law Center pointed out, that piece of legislation was "flushed away" later that year. But other states followed suit, including Texas, Nevada, Wisconsin, South Dakota, Tennessee, and, most prominently, North Carolina.

In the wake of legislation criminalizing trans people for using the bathroom consistent with their gender identitiy, a number of North Carolina individuals and businesses have come out in defense of transgender people. The NBA even made the decision to move its 2017 All-Star Game to New Orleans because of the bathroom law. In April 2016, the retail giant Target announced that staff and customers could use the bathroom corresponding with their gender identity. Later that year, a petition sponsored by the conservative American Family Association had gathered almost 1.5 million signatures from people promising to boycott the store. The boycott threat did not work.

Arguments against transgender people's access to bathrooms that match their gender identity almost always center on issues of safety. The claim is that transgender women, or those not genuinely trans but pretending to be so for malicious purposes, could sexually or otherwise physically assault cisgender women. Not only is this highly unlikely, but transgender women face enormous risks of violence and assault. The Office for Victims of Crime reports that half of transgender people are sexually assaulted or sexually abused during their lives. This number is even higher for trans youth, trans people of color, and trans people who are homeless. The Williams Institute reports that 70 percent of transgender people surveyed have been denied access, verbally harassed, or physically assaulted in public restrooms. For some trans people, every time they walk into a restroom they are putting themselves at risk.

One commonly held misconception is that without anti-trans "bathroom bills," they are "free-for-alls" in which anyone can claim a trans identity and have access to spaces where people are vulnerable so as to perpetrate sexual assault. But restrooms are among the most highly scrutinized places in our communities. Gender-nonconforming people, whether trans or not, are routinely stared at, verbally harassed, and even physically removed from bathrooms. In New York City, during the 2007 Pride parade, a cisgender woman named Kadijah Farmer used the restroom in a West Village restaurant. A security guard entered the bathroom and began pounding on the stall door, insisting that Farmer leave and refusing her offers to show ID. In Detroit in 2015, a cisgender woman named Cortney Bogorad was pushed out of a restaurant bathroom by a security guard who insisted she was a man and then was forcibly removed from the restaurant. Both Farmer and Bogorad filed lawsuits. Most people targeted by gendered bathroom policing do not.

The focus in bathroom debates has primarily been on transgender women and not transgender men. Bathroom cultures differ by gender, and women's bathrooms tend to be places of more scrutiny than men's bathrooms. However, trans men in men's bathrooms often worry that if they are discovered, they could be physically or sexually assaulted. Many trans men experience anxiety using urinals or while waiting for a stall.

Proponents of bathroom bills often do not consider that forcing transgender people to use the bathroom matching their birth certificate can also cause many awkward moments. Michael Hughes, a muscled, bearded trans man from Minnesota, started a campaign taking selfies in women's bathrooms and posting them on social media with messages like "Do I look like I belong in a women's bathroom?" Similarly, Kelly Lauren, a prominent, very feminine transgender woman and performer, posted pictures surrounded by men using urinals with the caption "Houston, do you REALLY want me in the same restroom as your husband or boyfriend?" While both these people were using dramatic images as forms of activism, such uncomfortable, potentially dangerous situations for transgender people would occur countless times daily should such legislation pass.

The bulk of criticism about trans people using bathrooms is directed at trans women. It often focuses on their potentially being sexual predators who would target cisgender women and children. Fears of trans women as sexual predators stem from myths about trans women transitioning for sexual gratification. Trans men, on the other hand, are often assumed to transition in order to obtain the privileges of male status in a patriarchal society. These assumptions about trans women's and men's respective reasons for transition are a reflection of how we as a society value masculinity and devalue femininity.

Many contend that the debates about bathroom bills are not about trans people at all but, in fact, mostly about cisgender men. Proponents of bathroom bills frequently discuss the danger of "men" using women's bathrooms to lure and attack women. They argue that allowing trans people to use the restroom matching their gender identity will lead to men dressing up as women in order to prey on them. In September 2016, the American Family Association, which organized the Target boycott, published a blog post titled "10 Examples of Men Abusing Target's Dangerous Policy." At least nine of the ten examples listed are clearly cisgender men, most accused of taking photos or videos from under or over a stall door in a women's bathroom. Legislation criminalizing sexual assault already exists.

A December 2016 study published in the journal *Gender Issues* confirmed that cisgender men were the ones expressing this concern, finding that cisgender women were approximately four times more likely to state that "transgender women do not directly cause their safety and privacy concerns."

According to the Sexual Assault Awareness and Prevention Center at the University of Michigan, 99 percent of sex offenders in single-victim incidents are men. Women spend much of their mental energy on a daily basis thinking about ways to keep themselves safe. Given the intense social policing of bathrooms, dressing up as a woman to stealthily enter a women's bathroom is one of the most difficult ways to find victims. Reducing sexual violence, regardless of the identity of the perpetrator, is a goal of society as a whole. Further discriminating against transgender women, already some of the most vulnerable, is a misdirection of effort.

For transgender people, just going to a public bathroom—something all of us may need to do multiple times a day—can be extremely frightening. In the wake of numerous state bathroom bills, many transgender people have contributed to the hashtag #WeJust-NeedToPee. A Human Rights Watch (HRW) report focusing on trans youth and sex-segregated school facilities reveals that preventing youth from using bathrooms and locker rooms consistent with their gender identity leads to numerous health and safety issues. A fourteen-year-old transgender girl in Texas who was forced to use the boys' locker room was assaulted by a group of football players. A fifteen-year-old trans boy in Utah told HRW, "I just don't go to the bathroom at school," and another said, "I go home for lunch and use the bathroom there. And I don't go for the rest of the day."

Avoiding fluid intake or holding your bladder can lead to dehydration, urinary-tract infections, and kidney problems. In the HRW report, the mother of another transgender boy in Utah stated: "He told us about junior high and not going to the bathroom all day. He was getting bladder infections and we didn't know why." While the Department of Justice and the Department of Education have announced that Title IX of the Educational Amendments of 1972 protects transgender students' rights to use the facilities corresponding with their gender identity, a number of states have sued to challenge the federal government's interpretation.

Fighting anti-trans legislation in schools and other public spaces is important. But there are a number of smaller changes we can make as individuals or as members of organizations or companies to improve bathroom access for transgender people. Single-stall, gender-neutral restrooms can be beneficial not only for trans and gender-nonconforming people but also for families and people with disabilities. In larger, multi-stall restrooms that cannot currently be converted to single bathrooms, urinals can be removed and stalls upgraded for complete door and side coverage, so that people of all genders can be invited in. Work can also be done to change the language of bathroom access, acknowledging that many people, including trans people, require more access rather than less.

Trans People Are Mentally Ill and Therapy Can Change Them

Are trans people confused, delusional, deranged . . . or just plain crazy? Can we be made to be "un-trans"?

Trans people are frequently viewed as unstable. Some imagine that our desire to change genders is a symptom of a larger dysfunction or a form of mental illness. Others argue that we would be able to simply let go of our feelings if properly "motivated"—that providers could, and *should*, encourage trans people to live according to our genders assigned at birth.

Since health providers first began working with trans people, some have advocated for treatment aimed at changing our gender identities to align with our genders assigned at birth. Though those providers and researchers are now in the minority, they remain stubbornly vocal.

The facts, however, are against them. Numerous studies have demonstrated that trans people are, in general, happier and more well-adjusted after transition, and that there is no form of therapy that is successful in making trans people "un-trans." Trans people do have increased rates of mental health issues, but studies clearly show this is a result of living in a transphobic society rather than being transgender.

Like women, people of color, and LGB people before us, transgender and gender-nonconforming people have a long history of being pathologized by the medical and mental health community. Trans identity, originally called "transsexualism," was first introduced into the American Psychiatric Association's *Diagnostic and Statistical Manual of Mental Disorders, Version III*, in 1980. The initial *DSM* diagnosis, almost always used to describe trans women, included those with a persistent desire to rid themselves of their genitals and to live according to the social norms of the "other" gender. It also suggested that these longings were virtually always present since childhood. The text did separate transsexualism from schizophrenia and other psychotic disorders; still, many providers cited the desire to rid oneself of fully functioning body parts and the belief in oneself as not being the gender assigned at birth to be clear indications of severe mental illness.

The inclusion of trans identities in the *DSM* firmly established that the mental health community deemed "trans-ness" as a condition to be "fixed." In version four of the *DSM*, published in 1994, the diagnosis was changed to "gender identity disorder." This term still defined trans identity as something other than the norm—something different, problematic, and in need of corrective treatment.

Early versions of the World Professional Association for Transgender Health's (WPATH) Standards of Care also considered transition to be a last resort that might help those few individuals otherwise unable to live within society the possibility of a "successful" life. Those who were trans-identified were only permitted access to care once they had proven to the satisfaction of a team of specialists that they were truly trans. It was up to the provider to determine if the person's condition was severe enough to justify the radical step of transition.

More recently, trans people have taken it upon themselves to force change. Responding in part to pressure from trans and LGBQ activists, version five of the *DSM*, published in 2013, now contains the diagnosis "gender dysphoria." Though the new diagnosis remains in a manual of disorders, the term is more palatable to some, and the diagnosis it represents is more inclusive of gender-nonconforming people who do not fit into the gender binary. Simultaneously, transgender activism has driven the Standards of Care to be more flexible and somewhat more supportive of the full diversity of trans communities.

The presence of trans identities in the *DSM* continues to be controversial. There is a powerful movement to have gender-related diagnoses removed altogether, as some feel that any mental health diagnosis is stigmatizing and continues to pathologize trans identities. Others argue that the inclusion has benefits, most importantly insurance coverage. Still, many insurance companies continue to categorically exclude coverage for transition-related care, whether there is a diagnosis for it or not. The *International Classification of Diseases*, used in many countries around the world, is a separate listing of health conditions, and the eleventh edition of the *ICD*, expected in 2018, proposes the new diagnosis, "gender incongruence," which would be a non–mental health diagnosis and potentially less pathologizing, but which would allow for reimbursement of care.

Trans people have been historically stigmatized not only by the mental health community through the *DSM* but also by individual mental health providers. In 1979, Jon K. Meyer, under the direction of Paul McHugh, chair of the Johns Hopkins University psychiatry department, published a paper in which he wrote that transgender women who had undergone surgery at Johns Hopkins demonstrated "no significant improvement" over those who had been rejected from services. McHugh was outspoken about his political mission to close the Hopkins gender clinic—arguably the most important in the country—and to cease services for transgender people out of a personal belief that transgender people were inherently mentally ill.

Meyer's study resulted in the closure of transgender clinics across the country, and ultimately very few places remained where transgender people could get legitimate care. Countless people suffered; denied treatment, they felt rejected, lived lives of despair, and turned to illicit treatment via black market sources or continued to suffer the torment of dysphoria. Through McHugh, the erroneous belief spread that transgender people were resigned to be depressed, anxious, and unsuccessful members of society, and that high numbers committed suicide post transition.

Not surprisingly, it was later revealed that the Johns Hopkins study was severely flawed. Meyer argued that his results showed that trans people were no better off after transition, but the measures he used to assess success included value judgments such as whether they were in "gender-appropriate" relationships. This "research" has been widely disproven.

Amazingly, despite the current vibrancy and strength of the transgender community, McHugh continues to argue that trans people should not be supported in transitioning. Unfortunately, respected news sources such as the *Wall Street Journal* continue to publish his opinions. In March 2016, McHugh coauthored a position statement for a group called the American College of Pediatricians, an organization of physicians much smaller than the well-known American Academy of Pediatrics that uses its official sounding name to spread misinformation about transgender people. The statement paints trans people as mentally ill: "A person's belief that he or she is something they are not is, at best, a sign of confused thinking. When an otherwise healthy biological boy believes he is a girl, or an otherwise healthy biological girl believes she is a boy, an objective psychological problem exists that lies in the mind not the body, and it should be treated as such."

Even though McHugh's work has been discredited—as the last gasps of someone with very little relevance—his notions persist. Many practitioners with the misguided belief that "trans-ness" can and ought to be "cured" advocate a philosophy of care known as "conversion" or "reparative" therapy. Using coercion, manipulation, aversion therapy, and peer pressure, this form of treatment is designed to compel people to live heteronormative cisgender lives. These efforts have never been effective and have been strongly rejected as unethical by the American Psychiatric and Psychological Associations, American Academy of Pediatrics, American Academy of Child and Adolescent Psychiatry, and many other major organizations. Still, the efforts persist.

For example, for many years, Ken Zucker, a psychologist formerly with the Centre for Addiction and Mental Health (CAMH) in Toronto, was accused of practicing reparative therapy on gender-nonconforming children. His gender program was harshly criticized by clients and community members for enforcing outdated protocols that pressured transgender people to live as their assigned genders, being unwilling to engage with transgender and gender-nonconforming communities, and allowing only those who had "failed" to successfully live as their assigned genders to transition. It appears that CAMH's board of directors rightly agreed: Zucker was removed from his position at CAMH and the gender program was shuttered in 2015 pending review. Zucker continues to speak at conferences on transgender issues often over the outcry of the community itself, but his influence may be waning: one of Zucker's two lectures at the US Professional Association for Transgender Health conference in February 2017 was canceled due to protests.

The good news is that supportive mental health providers are increasing in number. In addition to major mental health associations rejecting reparative therapy, a number of US states and Canadian provinces are calling for or have passed legislation making these techniques illegal when working with minors.

Though being trans is not in itself a mental illness, transgender communities bear a disproportionate burden of mental illness. LGBTQ+ people are nearly three times more likely to experience mental illnesses such as major depression and generalized anxiety disorder than others, and those numbers are even higher in trans communities. It is well documented that fear of coming out and being discriminated against for one's sexual orientation or gender identity can lead to depression, post-traumatic stress disorder, and substance abuse. Trans people have significantly higher rates of smoking, obesity, and diabetes, physical health disparities that likely result from mental health issues such as depression.

For some, the agony of living in a body and assuming a role they feel is not genuine can be too overwhelming to bear. Lifetime suicide attempt rates among transgender people are shockingly high—possibly up to almost 43 percent, compared to just 1.6 percent of the general population.

This data is all consistent with minority stress models, which argue that ongoing exposure to discrimination, stigma, and sociocultural hostility drives poorer mental health outcomes, and that transgender and gender-nonconforming people are especially vulnerable. Increasingly, studies clearly show that it is society's lack of acceptance that leads to mental health issues, and not being trans itself.

Although we may understand the cause, this does not take away from the fact that trans people have elevated rates of depression, anxiety, substance abuse, self-harming behaviors like cutting, and suicidality, and that treatment is essential. Unfortunately, many trans people who seek help for mental health or substance abuse issues find that they face discrimination and harassment even within settings where the goal is to improve mental health. In a 2007 study of transgender people in substance abuse programs, 60 percent reported being required to use sleeping and shower facilities that did not match their gender, and many described verbal abuse from staff and other patients. Over a third of participants reported that they had stopped going to these programs because of transphobia.

In many instances, even if a mental health program is ostensibly supportive, the staff may have little training in transgender-specific issues. Fifty percent of respondents in the National Transgender Discrimination Survey reported having to teach their providers about transgender care. There are a number of mental health providers with experience working with trans populations. Some work within LGBTQ+ health centers, which often, but not always, provide sensitive and competent transgender care; others have private practices. Many psychiatrists with this background are members of the Association of LGBTQ Psychiatrists. Psychologists may be part of Division 44 of the American Psychological Association, and the National Association of Social Workers has a committee on LGBT issues. The World Professional Association for Transgender Health and GLMA: Health Professionals Advancing LGBT Equality are two organizations open to health professionals of any kind who are interested in transgender health. Many of these associations provide online tools to search for providers by geographic area.

There are also targeted programs in some cities to assist LGBTQ+ people who are struggling with specific mental health issues. For example, Callen-Lorde Community Health Center in New York City runs dialectical behavior therapy (DBT) groups for LGBTQ+ people looking to develop improved coping skills, especially if they have a history of trauma. Rainbow Heights Club, in Brooklyn, New York, is a psychosocial club that hosts meals, activities, and groups for LGBTQ+ people with severe mental illnesses such as schizophrenia and bipolar disorder.

In addition to formal mental health care, there are other strategies that have been shown to promote resilience in transgender people. Helping parents with gender-nonconforming children learn to be supportive can have a significant impact. In a 2010 study by the Family Acceptance Project, LGBTQ+ young adults with high levels of family acceptance showed greater levels of self-esteem and general health and lower levels of depression, substance abuse, and suicidal ideation and attempts. A 2016 study on the mental health of transgender children clearly demonstrated that "out" trans youth living in supportive environments with supportive families, schools, and friends have no greater rates of depression and anxiety than youth in similar environments who do not identify as trans. In addition to environmental changes that can be made to assist trans people in building resilience from a young age, trans people often engage in behaviors that build their capacity to thrive in difficult situations. Studies of transgender people's strategies for coping and resilience show that they often use techniques like positive reframing and self-talk, and turn to hobbies, humor, and spirituality to deal with transphobia in society. They also find ways to act as mentors to younger people, boosting their own and their mentees' sense of agency.

Transition-related health care also promotes resilience. The data are clear: when we have support, we thrive. Several recent studies have made it unambiguous that quality of life for transgender people is overwhelmingly improved after transition, and that transgender and gender-nonconforming people allowed to live in their self-identified genders do far better emotionally and physically. A 2010 meta-analysis of twenty-eight studies showed that 78 percent of transgender people reported significant improvement in psychological symptoms and 80 percent in quality of life with hormonal transition. A follow-up systematic review in 2016 confirmed that results from studies released since 2010 continued to show benefits. Numerous studies have demonstrated similar improvements with surgery, when it is desired. In a 2015 Italian study, transgender people who had undergone gender-affirming surgeries reported a similar quality of life to cisgender people, when matched by age, marital status, and educational level.

Starting hormonal therapy during the teen years, when appropriate, can also have positive effects. A 2014 study of trans teens in the Netherlands showed that those who were treated in puberty had similar psychological function to cisgender teens the same age.

According to the 2011 Transition Survey by Gender Advocacy Training and Education, 94 percent of trans people show an improvement in their quality of life and 96 percent in their sense of well-being with transition.

All this suggests that trans people are happier and more well-adjusted post transition, and that it is social stigma and lack of acceptance that lead to depression, anxiety, and suicidality, not being trans itself. If anything, our mental health improves with transition.

Getting Hormones and Surgery Is Easy

Imagine a society in which hormones are available at convenience stores and surgical clinics are as common as pizzerias, where people can change their legal name and gender at a local ATM-like kiosk. This is a world some fear we live in.

Those who believe that hormones and surgery are too easy to obtain worry that transition is becoming a fad, and that those who transition—especially children and young adults—may end up regretting their decisions.

At the same time, there are others who view our current system as too restrictive. They cite the multiple hoops that transgender people have to jump through—which often include psychiatric visits and referral letters—as prohibitive and argue that access is often limited to those with means.

In its early years, transition-related care was overseen by paternalistic physicians who viewed themselves as the best judges of what was likely to help their patients. Transgender clients, on the other hand, often viewed such providers as gatekeepers, standing in the way of much-needed resources. Today, many providers remain in gatekeeper roles, but as university gender programs have shuttered and LGBTQ+ health centers have assumed the role of health-care deliverers to this population, this has begun to change.

Many clinics and individual providers now use an Informed Consent model for the provision of hormones, a philosophy that Callen-Lorde describes as "a cooperative effort between patient and provider. . . . Patients who are well informed have a right to make their own decisions." Informed Consent is an empowered approach to treatment in which risks and benefits are discussed and individuals retain the authority to make decisions about their own life and health care. Concerns such as uncontrolled substance use, extreme psychiatric instability, or memory problems sometimes warrant further evaluation, but this philosophy of care radically shifts the power dynamic from one in which the provider has authority over a client to one in which client and provider are peers. Clients are seen as having the authority to determine what might be best for their lives and are understood to have full rights to body autonomy.

In major cities with large LGBTQ+ health centers, obtaining hormones can sometimes (but not always) be relatively smooth; however, in rural areas it can often be difficult to find knowledgeable providers. A 2011 study published by Stanford University researchers in the *Journal of the American Medical Association* found that, on average, medical schools spend only five hours over the entire four years of study on education about LGBTQ+ health concerns, resulting in few physicians with any knowledge about transgender health. Lack of health insurance is another barrier to obtaining hormones, but even many employer-sponsored health plans specifically exclude transition-related care, and most state Medicaid programs do not cover hormones or surgeries.

Gender-affirming surgeons are often conservative, following the World Professional Association for Transgender Health guidelines and typically requiring one or two letters of recommendation (depending on the type of procedure) from a mental health or primary care provider before proceeding. The current version of the WPATH Standards of Care is meant to be flexible, but many surgeons fear they would be opening themselves up to liability if they did not follow the guidelines strictly. It can be time consuming and expensive for trans people to obtain multiple letters of reference. In addition, gender-related surgeries range in price, but many are expensive and out of reach financially for the majority of trans people.

Even with the numerous steps that trans people are required to take in order to gain access to hormones and surgeries, critics of current practices still argue that they are too easy to obtain. One of the biggest concerns is that those seeking hormones or surgery will regret the decision later on, but decades-long follow-up studies conducted by researchers around the world demonstrate extremely low regret rates (0–3 percent).

Many are concerned about these health-care interventions being applied to children, unaware that children do not physically transition with hormones or surgeries. Instead, children who express gender-nonconforming behaviors or thoughts and have supportive parents often work with therapists to explore their feelings, and some socially transition, adopting clothes, hairstyles, names, and pronouns that they feel fit them. There are times when children socially transition and then later decide that the gender they were assigned at birth actually fits more comfortably, and these individuals, in supportive environments, still thrive. The distress often experienced is more commonly due to an intolerant social atmosphere; it is more harmful to prevent children from exploring their gender identities than to follow them on their journeys, wherever they may lead.

Some adolescents are prescribed hormone blockers, which can be offered in the early stages of puberty to halt the development of secondary sex characteristics, or even later in puberty to prevent ongoing body changes and menstrual cycles, or to provide time for an individual to make decisions. However, hormone blockers are extremely expensive and financially prohibitive for most families. Teenagers with supportive families may have the option to start adult hormones like estrogen or testosterone if they are mature enough to understand their decisions.

Our current approaches to care for transgender people seeking hormones or surgeries are less restrictive than they were in the past, but far from making it too easy to obtain hormones and surgeries, these systems continue to put up numerous barriers. Unfounded fears related to regret rates, which are actually quite low, continued to drive opposition to efforts to increase access and make it harder for trans people to live as their authentic selves.

MYTH 16

Testosterone Makes You Angry and Estrogen Makes You Emotional

Searching YouTube for the word "transgender" yields more than a million results, many of which are personal "before and after" photo lineups or time-lapse videos of transition. YouTube and social networking sites like Facebook and Instagram allow trans people to document the experience themselves and to share the changes with their friends, family, other trans people, and the general public. Much of this material focuses on physical transformation, but other posts document the psychological experience of transition—the joy, the sadness, the frustration, and often the peace that result from a decision to take a leap.

Emotional changes during transition vary considerably. Relief is common, as is decreased depression and anxiety. Some trans men report feeling more angry or irritable after starting testosterone or find they can't cry as easily. Trans women on estrogen or progesterone sometimes feel their mood shifts more easily or that they're tearful at times when they might not have been before. Because there are so few studies of the emotional effects of hormones during transition, most of what we know is anecdotal, and it's hard to say which experiences are most common. In a culture that expects men and women to conform to gender norms, it's important to question if we expect (and, in turn, pay more attention to) hormonal effects that match what we think those hormones will do.

Testosterone is associated with masculinity and evokes images of muscle-clad young men pounding weights, soldiers going off to war, anger, fights, and sexual prowess. Estrogen and progesterone, on the other hand, are associated with femininity and call to mind a sense of comfort, warmth, motherly love, and kindness. We also think of them as causing stereotypically female emotional responses, like mood swings and tearfulness. Without scientific studies, we don't know if most people who transition experience hormones in these ways. Even *with* studies, we may never know if all the effects of transitional hormones are directly related to the hormones themselves or whether our beliefs about how they will affect us end up shaping the way we experience them.

The concept that chemical messengers could travel through the body to affect organs remote from their source originated in ancient China. However, it wasn't until the 1930s that researchers were able to isolate hormones such as testosterone and estrogen in order to use them medicinally. These two hormones in particular became known as "sex hormones" and entered into popular culture as symbols of masculinity and femininity. However, everyone's body, regardless of biological sex or gender identity, produces both of these chemicals. Though the typical male range for testosterone is higher than the typical female range, and vice versa for estrogen (until menopause), testosterone is not an exclusively "male" hormone and estrogen is not exclusively "female."

Many people are surprised to learn that estrogen is produced by cells in the testicles and that the chemical structure of testosterone and estrogen is similar, so much so that it takes only one enzyme (aromatase) to convert testosterone to estrogen. Not only are these hormones present in everyone's bodies, but their functions are not limited to sex and reproduction. Among other things, testosterone helps build muscle mass and increases the production of red blood cells, and estrogen improves bone health and cholesterol levels.

What does all this mean for transgender people who decide to take hormones as part of transition? What kinds of effects should they expect? Most commonly, transgender men take testosterone to transition. In the United States, injectable testosterone is frequently used, though patches and gels are also available. Within the first month or two, the menstrual cycle stops. Over the first six months, many trans men begin to have more oily skin and may develop acne. Then they may start to see facial hair, as well as increased body hair, and they may experience their voice "cracking" and then lowering permanently. Muscle and fat distribution can change significantly, and it can be easier to build muscle mass. Some trans men notice the emergence of male pattern baldness, which, depending on age, can happen very quickly during transition. Testosterone levels do not always have to be monitored if the desired effects are occurring. However, there can be some rare, serious side effects, such as a thickening of the blood due to increased red blood cells.

Reproductive issues for trans men became news in 2007 with the public story of Thomas Beatie, "the pregnant man." Though he may be the most famous, many other transgender men have also given birth. It is possible to become pregnant by accident while on testosterone, though this is unlikely because ovulation is usually shut down. Trans men should be careful that fertilization does not happen because testosterone is a pregnancy category X medication, meaning that it can cause damage to the growing fetus. Many trans men desiring to become pregnant stop using testosterone and wait for the return of their menstrual cycle. This has resulted in many healthy babies.

In terms of the emotional effects of testosterone, what is true for one trans man may not be true for another. Some do experience increased anger or irritability when starting testosterone, but others report the opposite—feeling calmer. There are, on the other hand, studies that confirm another belief about taking testosterone: it is well documented that trans men first starting testosterone often experience an increase in libido (sexual arousal). Most importantly, across multiple studies in many areas of the world, trans men report increased quality of life and decreases in depression, anxiety, and suicide rates on testosterone.

Trans women starting hormonal transition have a few choices. Most trans women who will not or have not yet had vaginoplasty (i.e., surgery that transforms a penis and scrotum into a vulva, clitoris, labia, and vaginal canal) take both estrogen and an anti-androgen medication. Anti-androgens are meant to block the effects of hormones such as testosterone, which is still produced by the testicles even while on estrogen. The most common anti-androgen in the United States is a pill called spironolactone. Estrogen comes in various forms, including pills, patches, and injections. Together, estrogen and an anti-androgen can help to smooth the skin, redistribute the body fat and muscle ratio in a more feminine pattern, decrease body hair, and cause breast growth, but they do not stop the growth of facial hair or increase the pitch of the voice. They also do not generally improve male pattern baldness if that has already occurred. In addition to estrogen and spironolactone, a minority of trans women also take progesterone. There has been some debate over whether progesterone provides additional benefit, and most studies suggest that it does not.

For trans women on hormones, counterintuitively, testosterone levels are often tracked to make sure they have decreased to within the female range. It is also important to follow the potassium level while on the anti-androgen spironolactone because it can become dangerously high under certain circumstances. The most well-known serious side effect from estrogen treatment is the development of blood clots, which often start in the legs and can move to the lungs (pulmonary embolism), causing respiratory failure and death. Trans women who smoke can lower their risk of blood clots by cutting down or quitting. Both testosterone and estrogen use can, in some cases, severely impact cholesterol and triglyceride levels, and these should be monitored closely.

Although trans women with children have not featured as prominently in major news sources, many do have biological offspring. Often, their children were "fathered" before the women medically transitioned. Once trans women start on estrogen and anti-androgens, their sperm production and ability to have children decreases. These changes may be irreversible. For many people, this is a desired effect of taking hormones. However, others delay taking hormones or choose sperm banking prior to starting hormones and later have children with womb-bearing partners.

Like the stereotypes about testosterone, there are myths about the effects of estrogen. Many trans women expect that they will become more emotional or tearful when they start taking estrogen, and though some report these feelings, others do not. As with testosterone, "your mileage may vary." Many trans women also report that their sex drive decreases, although some say the opposite—that they experience more sexual feelings, not fewer, and often attribute this to finally getting to be who they are. Most studies of trans women and hormones have focused on psychological health and demonstrate comparable increases in quality of life and decreases in depression, anxiety, and suicidality to testosterone in trans men.

Some trans people, many of whom identify as genderqueer and don't fit into the categories of trans man or trans woman, may want to take hormones that will allow them to look androgynous or to have certain characteristics but not others. Some people take lower dose hormones or take hormones for a short time and then stop. Many are happy with the results. Unfortunately, the effects can be unpredictable, and the outcome may be a combination of both desired and undesired effects.

The unsupervised use of hormones carries risk. Taking higher than advised doses of either testosterone or estrogen, with the hopes that the effects will occur faster, is known to cause emotional instability and an increase in side effects, as well as a variety of health issues, such as increased risk for blood clots.

Though no such experience is universal, trans people taking hormones at prescribed doses do very well emotionally. Some trans men do experience feeling more angry and some trans women cry more, but just as many people seem to have the opposite reactions. A common refrain that comes both from trans men and trans women is "I feel more calm" or "I feel more like myself." The studies that do exist related to the emotional effects of hormones are limited (one to two hundred people per study). However, they seem to show that overall psychological functioning, anxiety, depression, and quality of life are improved on hormones. Because these studies are small, they don't tell us much about the more subtle effects that these treatments may have. Hopefully, increasing interest in transgender health may generate more research grants in this area. What we do know is that trans people are generally satisfied with their choice to take hormones, and that hormones such as testosterone and estrogen are just part of what makes us masculine and feminine.

MYTH 17

Laws Support Trans People

After six years of serving her community, the Detroit funeral home employee Aimee Stephens was fired when she came out as transgender. A federal court upheld her employer's right to terminate her. Kansas resident Stephanie Mott requested to change her gender on her birth certificate and was told that even if she had genital surgery, state law does not allow her to amend the document. Virginia high school student Gavin Grimm transitioned during his sophomore year, and by senior year he was still not allowed to use the boys' bathroom at his public school. These cases, all of which occurred between 2013 and 2016, underscore the fact that though transgender awareness has increased in both the media and among Americans in general, some laws still lag behind. Final edits to this book were made in February 2017, shortly after Donald Trump became president. It remains to be seen how the current or future administrations will affect transgender people under the law.

From a young age, transgender and gender-nonconforming people suffer from a lack of legal protections. There are no federal laws that explicitly protect transgender students against discrimination at school. Title IX of the Education Amendments of 1972, however, states that "no person in the United States shall, on the basis of sex, be excluded from participation in, be denied the benefits of, or be subjected to discrimination under any education program or activity receiving Federal financial assistance." Title IX has been interpreted by some lawyers as applying to transgender students. In 2016, in the wake of North Carolina's "bathroom bill" preventing people from using public bathrooms corresponding with their gender, the Obama administration sent a letter to every school district in the country advising them to use students' preferred names and pronouns and to allow the use of bathrooms and locker rooms matching students' gender identities. This letter is not law, but as a directive from the president, it carries a threat of lawsuits or loss of federal funding for schools that do not comply.

As they become adults, trans people face barriers at every level when it comes to employment. They are less likely to have family support and access to higher education, less likely to be hired and more likely to be let go. Their unemployment rate is twice the national average, and for black trans people, four times the average. Some things have shifted; in 2014, President Obama signed an executive order prohibiting federal contractors from discriminating on the basis of sexual orientation or gender identity. In addition, some federal courts have interpreted the Equal Protection Clause of the Fourteenth Amendment as applying to transgender people, arguing that anti-trans discrimination is a form of sex discrimination and allowing recourse for transgender people who have been wrongfully terminated to seek justice. However, this still leaves most transgender people without assured job protection.

Eighteen US states and more than 130 cities ban discrimination based on gender identity, including employment discrimination, but no law protects trans people on a federal level. The Employment Nondiscrimination Act (ENDA), a proposed federal law that would make it illegal to fire or fail to hire or promote a person due to sexual orientation or gender identity, was first introduced in Congress in 1994. In 2007, there was significant controversy surrounding ENDA when Democrats, supported by some LGBTQ+ organizations, including the Human Rights Campaign (HRC), suggested that the legislation move forward without protection based on gender identity.

They argued that ENDA was unlikely to pass without the change, but this lack of solidarity and willingness to dismiss the needs of a significant part of the LGBTQ+ community resulted in a feeling of betrayal on behalf of many people.

Housing discrimination is also a significant issue for many transgender people. Fortunately for those in public housing projects, in shelters, and on federally funded voucher programs such as Section 8, federal regulations do explicitly prohibit discrimination based on gender identity and sexual orientation. However, despite legal protections, there are still high levels of discrimination. Because of family rejection and social stigma, approximately one-fifth of trans people experience homelessness at some point in their lives. The same percentage report being refused a home or apartment because of their gender identity. More than half of trans people who try to access shelters report being harassed by staff or other residents; 29 percent say they have been turned away, and 22 percent describe being sexually assaulted by staff or residents. For those who rent or buy their homes outside the public system, at least twenty states and two hundred cities and counties prohibit discrimination in housing, although, just as in the public system, there are gaps between laws and outcomes.

Appallingly, many people in our country are housed in the US prison system. The United States has 4.4 percent of the world's population and 22 percent of the global prison population. Sixteen percent of transgender people overall and 47 percent of black transgender people have been incarcerated at some point in their lives, often on charges related to sex work or other nonviolent, survival-related crimes. According to the Federal Bureau of Justice Statistics, 40 percent of transgender prisoners are sexually abused in any given year. Transgender people in jails and prisons have few legal protections. Though federal guidelines mandate that decisions on where to place inmates not be based solely on their external genitalia, trans women are still often held in men's prisons. There they may be segregated, ostensibly for their own protection, into cells where they spend twenty-three hours a day alone. Many transgender people are refused access to hormonal or surgical treatments while in custody. The Department of Justice has issued statements requiring state prisons to provide prisoners with hormone treatment if they were receiving it before incarceration, but this directive is routinely ignored. Trans people who were not yet on hormones prior to incarceration have even less recourse. And there is almost no way for someone to access surgery from prison. This may soon change, though, because in 2015, after a trans woman named Shiloh Quine filed a lawsuit, California became the first state to agree to an inmate's gender-affirming surgery.

Family law is another area in which transgender people have had difficulty with discrimination. Transgender people have lost child-custody and visitation cases, and have been prevented from adopting or had their adoptions invalidated because of their transgender status. (See Myth 12, "Trans People Are a Danger to Others, Especially Children," for more information.)

Trans people face harassment and violence on a daily basis. Some activists and lawyers have proposed that adding "trans" as a category to hate crimes bills could potentially prevent attacks or at least provide recourse. Such legislation can increase law enforcement investigation into, and also penalties for, crimes committed based on hatred toward a particular group. In 2009, the United States passed a law that expanded the definition of federal hate crimes to include those motivated by sexual orientation and gender identity. Though some LGBTQ+ people supported this bill, others were wary of any law that would lengthen prison sentences, arguing that trans people are targeted by police and experience high rates of incarceration, and that, therefore, expanding the US prison system is not the answer to their problems. Similarly, trans people disagree on whether it is useful, or even moral, to fight for trans inclusion in the military. Some trans people are proud to be involved in the military or hope to someday serve their country in this way, while others feel the military is simply another patriarchal institution that should be dismantled.

In 2016, the Pentagon announced it was lifting the ban on service by transgender people in the US military. Transgender military personnel will also now be provided with transition-related health care. However, new recruits are expected to have transitioned at least eighteen months prior to starting service.

There are numerous controversies within trans communities about the best ways to use laws to improve the lives of trans people. In 2015, the Supreme Court legalized same-sex marriage in all fifty states. This was a historic moment that some believed would lead to increased LGBTQ+ rights legislation in many other ways, but it also represented the culmination of a period in which a large number of trans and queer people felt that the focus on marriage equality pushed aside other issues more important for the LGBTQ+ community. Many trans people, for example, continue to lack access to transition-related health care, while countless LGBQ+ people also have difficulty obtaining primary care or mental health care; discrimination is still rampant in housing, employment, and education; and many parts of the LGBTQ+ community face poverty, all of which leads some to argue that the resources devoted to marriage could have been better spent.

Health care in the United States is a confusing web of rules and regulations, and is subject to change by federal and local governments. Employer-sponsored health insurance often explicitly excludes any care that is considered part of transition, or it initially rejects claims, putting the burden on the already stigmatized enrollee to endure a lengthy and frustrating appeal process. The Affordable Care Act (often called Obamacare) of 2010 bans sex discrimination in federally subsidized health care, and guidelines interpret this as including discrimination against transgender people. The result is that Medicare, the federal health-care program for senior citizens; Medicaid, the federal-state health-care program for low-income people; and health insurance bought through state exchanges cannot discriminate. However, what discrimination means legally is debatable. These plans can no longer categorically exclude transition-related care nor deny services based on a person's transgender status. It remains unclear whether these programs are required to provide all medically necessary transition-related care. Medicare provides hormone therapy and, as of a 2014 ruling, also covers gender-affirming surgeries. Medicaid coverage varies from state to state, and most state programs do not pay for hormones or surgeries, although this is changing. A minority of states have passed legislation banning trans exclusions in insurance plans. These include California, Colorado, Illinois, Massachusetts, New York, Oregon, Pennsylvania, Rhode Island, Vermont, and Washington.

In almost every aspect of their lives, including school, work, travel, and interactions with law enforcement, trans people benefit from having identification documents that match their name and gender. One of the most difficult aspects of obtaining these documents is that many are regulated on a state level, and each state has different requirements. The requirements to change gender markers on driver's licenses, for example, vary from state to state. In some states, gender-affirming surgery is required for proof. In others, a letter from a physician stating that someone has medically transitioned will suffice.

States also have a variety of approaches to gender changes on birth certificates. Those seeking a new birth certificate must do so through the state in which they were born, and so some trans people, now living in progressive states, may be unable to change their birth certificates if they were born somewhere else, no matter what they do. Other states require hormonal or surgical transition. Some states will amend the original birth certificate, while others will issue a completely new one.

On a federal level, it has become easier for transgender people to obtain appropriate identification. In 2010, the State Department announced that gender-affirming surgery was no longer required to obtain a gender change on a passport. Surgery could be replaced by a letter from a physician stating that the person had undergone appropriate clinical treatment for gender transition. In 2013, the Social Security Administration also decided that proof of surgery was no longer required to make a gender change in their records and that either a physician's letter or the submission of a government-issued form of identification with the correct gender would be sufficient.

Legal protections for transgender people are steadily increasing, sometimes on a local level and other times through national legislation or guidelines. Sometimes the law lags behind social progress, while at other times it seems as if society can't keep pace. There are disagreements over the best ways to advance, from changing our current systems to accommodate transgender people to tearing those systems down and rebuilding them from the ground up. However we decide to effect change, our goal should be to move toward a better future for all people, including those who are transgender and gender nonconforming, and not lose sight of the most marginalized.

PART 4

HISTORY AND COMMUNITY

MYTH 18

Trans People Have Existed Throughout Time

Joan of Arc, born around 1412, is a French folk hero and Catholic saint, known for her role as a leader and military strategist as France fought England in the Hundred Years' War. For centuries she was viewed worldwide as an iconic woman warrior who dressed as a man. She wore men's clothes, it was argued, in order to move through enemy territory and because armor was necessary in battle. Since the 1970s, historians have researched the lives of LGBTQ+ people throughout time. Some, such as trans writer and activist Leslie Feinberg, have argued that Joan of Arc, among others, was an early gay or transgender pioneer.

Across cultures and throughout history, many people have defied gender stereotypes or taken on roles typically associated with another sex. A number of ancient societies, from Asia to the Middle East to Greece and Rome, included eunuchs, people assigned male at birth who were castrated and served specific social functions, often as servants, but sometimes as high-ranking officials. Eunuchs also worked as priests in temples devoted to goddesses. The *hijras* of South Asia have also existed for many centuries. Prior to European invasion, many North American native tribes included Two Spirits, gender-nonconforming people who often took on positions in their cultures that blended male and female roles. Since at least the fifteenth century, some Balkan families included Sworn Virgins, who were assigned female at birth but, after an oath of celibacy, took on the roles of a man.

While past societies have allowed or, in some cases, encouraged varied gender expressions, it is difficult to determine how closely aligned each might have been with today's understanding of transgender identity. Complicating things even more, a number of LGBTQ+ historians have argued that in some of these cultures, gender-bending served a primary purpose of allowing people to express same-sex desires and was not about gender itself.

It can be impossible to know how to categorize many individual historical figures. Often there are no written records that detail their inner lives or explain how they wished to be viewed. For others, it is clearer. Sarah Emma Edmonds and Albert Cashier were both assigned female at birth and fought for the Union army during the Civil War, but their stories reveal that their gender identities were likely significantly different. Edmonds enlisted as a man, but after near discovery, she deserted, later publishing a memoir called *Female Spy of the Union Army*, marrying a man, and having three children. Cashier, on the other hand, served until the end of the war, then returned home to Illinois, where he lived and worked as a man, collected his military pension, and even voted in elections. He was not discovered to have been assigned female until he developed dementia and entered a state hospital, where he was forced to wear a dress.

Researchers have discovered a number of other people in history believed to have lived similarly to transgender people today. Chevalier d'Eon was assigned male at birth in 1728 and worked as a French ambassador, soldier, spy, and expert swordsperson, sometimes dressing as a woman to infiltrate and gather information. In her fifties, d'Eon began to dress full time as a woman and petitioned the French government to recognize her as female. Willmer "Little Axe" Broadnax was a well-known gospel singer active in the 1940s to the 1960s. Until his death in 1992, his brother, fellow gospel singer Willie "Big Axe" Broadnax, was the only person who knew Willmer had been assigned female at birth.

Broadnax lived in an era when he and others might be aware of the idea that there were those who identified as transsexual or transvestites—some of the words of the time. Cashier and d'Eon, on the other hand, were much less likely to have had concepts of themselves that match our current thinking about gender identity, because the ideas we have today are relatively new. Would they have called themselves "transgender" if they were alive today? What about Native Americans like We'wha, who was born in 1849 into the Zuni tribe in New Mexico and was known as an *Ihamana*—someone who was assigned male at birth, dressed in both male and female clothing, and engaged in women's work as well as serving as a tribe mediator? We have no way of knowing how these people would have defined themselves through a modern lens, and it would be unfair to apply to them a label they did not use for themselves.

What we do know is that our terminology and understanding of gender identity in the Western world have shifted significantly over the last 150 years. The well-known transgender activist Sylvia Rivera (1951–2002) identified as transgender later in life, but earlier on she used a variety of terms to refer to herself, including "gay," "queen," "half-sister," and "transvestite."

How did today's understanding of transgender identity develop? Its history is intricately linked to the history of gay and lesbian identities. The gay historian John D'Emilio suggests that the rise of capitalism in the 1800s, accompanied by the shift from countryside family living to individual wage work in cities, was the catalyst for the eventual formation of the modern gay identity category. Before then, argued French philosopher Michel Foucault, though many people engaged in same-sex sexual activity, there was no category of people labeled "homosexual," either as a collective group or an identity. There was also no widespread concept of transgender identity or its precursors.

Early on in the development of gay and transgender identities as categories, the concepts of gender identity and sexuality as we understand them today were not clearly delineated. In 1868, for example, Karl Ulrichs published pamphlets that referred to men who were attracted to other men as "urnings." "The Urning," Ulrichs wrote, "is not a man, but rather a kind of feminine being," stressing that such men were "mentally" feminine.

Ulrichs was not alone in viewing sexual orientation as connected to ideas about gender. Nineteenth-century German psychiatrist Richard von Krafft-Ebing saw homosexuality and transgender identity as falling along a continuum from "only homosexual feeling and instinct, but limited to the sexual life," to "the whole psychical personality, and even the bodily sensations." At the turn of the twentieth century, the terms "invert" and "inversion" were commonly used as synonyms for homosexuality, but they were also used to describe a range of other behaviors, most often those that challenged gender norms. For many of these thinkers, gender identity and sexuality were initially viewed on a spectrum rather than as separate concepts.

By the beginning of the twentieth century, some people were beginning to distinguish between gay and transgender identities. British physician Havelock Ellis wrote of two "inverts" he saw for treatment that "one of them is of somewhat feminine nature generally; the other remains masculine in his non-sexual habits." In 1910, sexologist Magnus Hirschfeld published *Transvestites*, in which he wrote that "not all homosexuals are effeminate" and "not all effeminate men are homosexual." Most importantly, people who themselves identified as gender nonconforming were beginning to speak out. In 1918, Ralph Werther, writing as Earl Lind, and also known as Jennie June, published *Autobiography of an Androgyne*, in which she described a club she attended with other "androgynes" known as the Cercle Hermaphroditos.

The evolution of language is complicated, especially when it relates to identity. Until at least the 1940s, the term "transvestite" was used to refer to gender-nonconforming people who might today identify as transgender, as well as to cisgender people who cross-dressed for personal pleasure or as entertainers. Today we refer to those who cross-dress for entertainment as drag queens or kings; most, but not all, drag artists identify as cisgender.

In 1949, American sexologist David Cauldwell published an article titled "Psychopathia Transsexualis" and is credited with inventing the term "transsexual," which came to replace "transvestite" in the second half of the twentieth century. Since then, "transvestite" began to be understood solely as describing someone who enjoyed dressing in the clothing of another gender, but did not identify with that gender. (Today, such a person would be known as a cross-dresser.) "Transsexual" referred to someone whose gender identity differed from the one assigned at birth. Well into the 1970s, many people who would likely see themselves as transgender today called themselves transvestites. The term continues to be used pejoratively against transgender people.

The language we use today, including "transgender," "gender nonconforming," and "genderqueer," developed over the last few decades. The origin of the term "transgender" is debated. Some say that activist Virginia Prince first coined a variant on transgender—"transgenderist"—to describe people such as herself who identified with another gender but did not have surgical interventions. In the early 1990s, Holly Boswell and others began to use the term "transgender" to describe those who pushed the boundaries of gender and who refused to accept the binary gender system. Around the same time, "transgender" was first used as an umbrella term that included many people of varying identities, and because "transsexual" was increasingly viewed as a medicalized, stigmatizing term. Today, "transgender" is often used this way, although some people would instead use "gender nonconforming" for this purpose.

It is evident that, throughout history, gender-nonconforming people have been part of many societies, and that their gender identities and the ways they understood gender in general reflected their cultures and times. Placing a modern lens on their lives is not always possible or even helpful or appropriate. Language and ideas related to gender are constantly evolving and will continue to evolve. Conceptualizations of gender we hold as truths today will be seen as differently through the lens of future generations as those of our predecessors are to us.

Certain Cultures Universally Embrace Trans People

The *hijras* of India and *kathoeys* of Thailand. The *waria* of Indonesia and *muxe* of southern Mexico. The *fa'afafine* of Polynesia and Two Spirit people of Native American cultures. Scholars point to these groups as examples of gender-nonconforming people who are respected, even revered in their societies—and compare them to transgender and gender-nonconforming people in the mainstream United States, who face a complex mix of discrimination and support. News articles tout "7 Countries Giving Transgender People Fundamental Rights the US Still Won't," arguing that trans people in places such as India, Nepal, and Pakistan have respect not accorded to trans people in the United States. Are hijras and kathoeys better off than gender-nonconforming people in the United States? Did Native American tribes universally embrace Two Spirit people?

The answer to these questions is complicated. There are gender-nonconforming people all over the world, and each culture has a unique way of understanding the cultural role they play. Focusing on a few of these countries may help explain the diversity of experiences of gender-nonconforming people.

Hijras have existed for centuries in the region now known as India, Bangladesh, and Pakistan. References to a third sex—one other than male or female—exist in the texts of all three of India's ancient religions—Hinduism, Jainism, and Buddhism. The hijra population today may number five to six million and is generally made up of people assigned male at birth who express traits that are traditionally seen as feminine. Some identify as transgender women or simply as women, while others see the hijra role as a unique category outside the binary gender system. Hijras often live in groups together, with more senior hijras, known as *gurus*, running households and holding sway over geographic areas.

During the British colonization, a number of laws were passed to criminalize hijras. There is controversy over the status of hijras prior to colonialism, and it is likely that some were treated relatively well and others poorly. In 2014, the Indian Supreme Court ruled in favor of recognizing a third sex on all official documents. Does the establishment of a separate category for hijras demonstrate a more accepting attitude toward gender-nonconforming people in India than in countries such as the United States? Despite recent legal changes, the social status of hijras remains ambiguous. Though hijras are accepted as a part of Indian society, they are often disowned by their families, discriminated against in employment, and targeted for violence and abuse. Many hijras earn money doing sex work, and HIV has taken a large toll on hijra communities. In addition, the international news coverage citing legal improvements for hijras is misleading; until the 1990s, hijras could not vote at all, and in many Indian states, they continue to be denied the right to vote or run for public office unless they declare themselves either male or female. Though hijras are a longstanding part of Indian culture and have thriving communities, their lives are not simple or easy.

Thailand is often thought of by travelers as a place of relative acceptance for gender-nonconforming people. The term for people in Thailand with identities closest to transgender women in the United States is "kathoey," though this term is also used for intersex people and effeminate gay men. Kathoeys can, in some instances, be very successful. Well-known kathoeys include Nong Tum, whose life story was told in the film *Beautiful Boxer*, as well as the all-kathoey pop band Venus Flytrap. Life is not always easy for kathoeys, and they are sometimes the targets of sexual violence. Like hijras, many kathoeys are sex workers—some because they choose to be, and others because they have limited options.

In addition to kathoeys, Thailand has *toms*, who are assigned female at birth and present masculinely. Toms may wear masculine clothing and cut their hair short, and some bind their chests. Toms often date *dees* (the name "dee" comes from Thais pronouncing the end of the word "lady," i.e., "lay-dee"), who are generally more feminine. Some toms identify as lesbians and others as transgender men.

In the Balkans (primarily northern Albania) gender-nonconforming people have played a significant role throughout the region's history. "Sworn virgins" are assigned female at birth and raised as girls but take over the male role as head of household when no man is available. This lack of leadership occurs frequently because blood feuds between families are so common that many men within a single family may be killed. Sworn virgins agree to a vow of chastity but essentially take on all the privileges and responsibilities of men: owning property, socializing with other men, and carrying weapons. This tradition extends back at least five centuries and is believed to stem from the Kanun, a set of traditional Albanian laws that hold that women are worth half as much as men but female virgins are equal to men.

Experts believe that there are fewer than a hundred sworn virgins in the Balkans today, many of them elderly. One possible reason for this is that as Albanian women have gained social status, there is now less of a need for those assigned female to fill male roles. Sworn virgins report a diverse array of experiences and feelings, ranging from extreme satisfaction to wishes that they had not taken on their positions. Some understand themselves as men, while others feel they are not quite the same as men but are not women either. Many describe enjoying the social freedoms and privileges they have been given, while others mourn the loss of women's spaces and physical intimacy.

"Two Spirit" is an umbrella term adopted in 1990 by activists at the Third International Native Gay and Lesbian Gathering in Winnipeg, Canada, to describe gender-nonconforming people in Native American/First Nations communities. It replaced *"berdache,"* a derogatory term used by French clergy and explorers who encountered Native tribes.

There is documentation of gender-nonconforming people in hundreds of Native American, also known as First Nations, societies. Words used to describe these groups include *"Nadleeh"* (Navajo), *"Agokwa"* (Chippewa), *"Bote"* (Crow), and *"Winkte"* (Dakota), among many others. Not all Native American societies were universally accepting of gender nonconformity, and those that were often had prescribed expectations. In many tribes, gender-nonconforming people had specialized work activities or filled roles as healers or shamans. Many had sexual relationships with members of their assigned sex. Some wore clothing typical of another sex, while others did not. Historians argue that those we call Two Spirit today likely represent the entire LGBTQ+ spectrum and not just trans identities.

It should be noted that in modern days, many people not of First Nations heritage have adopted this label to describe their identity as containing both masculine and feminine elements, a use of language increasingly seen as inappropriate by Native Americans. A Native American blogger from the White Noise Collective writes that the term exists specifically within a First Nations context of oppression and cultural understandings of identity, and is not applicable to those outside this community: "If you are not a member of a First Nations tribe, then it is not liberatory to use the term 'Two Spirit.' If you did not descend from their ancestors and their struggles, and if you do not understand the history of their tribes or their words, then they are not yours to use and your use of the terms is theft, or what is called cultural appropriation."

Cultures across the world and through time have had complicated, individual understandings and ways of simultaneously supporting and failing to integrate gender nonconformity. At times, we form unrealistic views of the treatment of gender-nonconforming people in other cultures. Why is it so appealing to idealize them? Given the history of Westerners viewing native people of all continents as more primitive than Europeans, there is likely racial and ethnic prejudice at play. The "noble savage," which originated as a literary archetype in French novels, describes a person who has not yet been exposed to civilization and therefore remains pure or good. This is often attributed to Jean-Jacques Rousseau, although he expressed this idea and did not use the actual phrase. Viewing people in this light simultaneously applauds but also demeans their cultures, painting them as a return to a more "simple" society, fixed in time, and writing off their complex and dynamic histories. This view promotes the idea that respect and support for gender-nonconforming people is not possible in a complicated, modern society.

It is unclear the extent to which racialized views play into idealization of certain cultures and their treatment of gender-nonconforming people. There is much to be learned from studying the role of gender-nonconforming people in cultures outside of our own, but in order to truly gain from them we must dig below the surface to discover the nuances and contradictions that make them real.

Trans People and Feminists Don't Get Along

Over the last few years, articles have appeared in mainstream media emphasizing a division between feminist and transgender movements. They come with sensational titles like the 2014 *New Yorker* piece "What Is a Woman? The Dispute Between Radical Feminism and Transgenderism" and paint a picture of screaming matches, cyberbullying, and even physical violence. The recent spotlight on conflicts between these groups suggests that the clashes are both new and widespread, when, in reality, they have been ongoing for years and are limited to a small subset of feminists.

From the beginning, trans people have been involved in feminist movements, many making significant contributions. Sylvia Rivera, a Latina trans woman considered one of the founders of today's trans movement, famously became friends with cisgender radical feminists while involved in a 1970 sit-in at New York University for the early gay liberation movement. Accounts indicate that the women participated in consciousness-raising groups together. When Sylvia and her best friend, Marsha P. Johnson, created the platform for their organization, Street Transvestite Action Revolutionaries (S.T.A.R.), they demanded "a revolutionary peoples' government, where transvestites, street people, women, homosexuals, puerto ricans, indians, and all oppressed people are free."

Masculine-spectrum trans people have also been heavily involved in feminist causes. Leslie Feinberg, the trans author of *Stone Butch Blues*, who used the gender-neutral pronouns "ze" and "hir," proudly identified as socialist, unionist, anti-racist, and feminist. Among many other actions, ze was involved in reproductive-rights work, helping to organize community self-defense around an abortion clinic in Buffalo, New York, where a doctor had been killed.

Despite a number of close relationships, as early as the 1970s, there were also collisions between some feminists and trans people. Beth Elliott, a trans folk singer and activist, was involved in lesbian-feminist movements, serving as vice president of the San Francisco chapter of the Daughters of Bilitis. Elliott was on the organizing committee for the 1973 West Coast Lesbian Feminist Conference, and was scheduled to perform. However, a lesbian separatist group calling itself the Gutter Dykes protested her presence, calling her a man. Keynote speaker Robin Morgan followed suit, saying, "I will not call a male 'she,'" accusing Elliott of "leeching off women who have spent [sic] entire lives as women" and referring to Elliott as "an opportunist, an infiltrator, and a destroyer—with the mentality of a rapist." "We know what's at work when whites wear blackface," said Morgan. "The same thing is at work when men wear drag."

Anti-trans sentiment within some feminist groups intensified in the late 1970s when Olivia Records, a feminist-collective music label, was attacked for including trans woman Sandy Stone as a sound engineer. The verbal assaults continued until Stone resigned. A year later, Janice Raymond published *The Transsexual Empire: The Making of the She-Male*, targeting Stone individually and arguing, "All transsexuals rape women's bodies by reducing the real female form to an artifact, appropriating this body for themselves." Raymond's work made many trans people, especially trans women, wary of collaborating with feminist groups and added fuel to a growing fire.

The 1990s were a time of continued clashes but also one of a burgeoning transgender political movement. The Michigan Womyn's Music Festival, founded in 1975, had always been billed as catering to "women-born-women" as an overt way of excluding trans women, at least on paper (though some did attend). In 1991, trans attendee Nancy Burkholder was pressured to disclose whether she was trans, and when she refused, she was ejected. This led to demonstrations over the next few years, as well as the use of nearby land to establish "Camp Trans," a welcoming environment for all people, in protest.

The majority of those who identify as feminists and oppose transgender rights are part of what is called radical feminism, though many people who use that label do not hold these views. Anti-trans radical feminists are sometimes referred to as "trans-exclusionary radical feminists," or TERFs, members of a sub-movement that evolved out of second-wave feminism.

Feminism in the United States is generally considered to have undergone three waves (so far), although this is a gross oversimplification of a very complicated movement. The first wave took place in the 1800s and early 1900s, and led to women's suffrage. Second-wave feminism, which sprouted in the 1960s and 1970s, was a push for social equality for women and included challenging gender roles at home and at work, as well as fighting for abortion rights. Third-wave feminism, beginning in the 1990s, is often thought of as a reaction to second-wave feminism, which has been criticized, fairly and unfairly, for centering white heterosexual women and failing to take into account the multiple systems of oppression that contribute to women's experiences. The third wave attempts to introduce the concept of intersectionality, which is the idea that patriarchy is not the only system of oppression that women face, and that all people have their own intersecting identities, including race, sexuality, immigration status, socioeconomics, and ability, that influence their lives.

As an example of intersectionality, trans author Julia Serano coined the term "transmisogyny" to refer to the unique discrimination experienced by transgender women, something similar to misogyny directed toward cisgender women. Serano argues that both are rooted in the belief that maleness and masculinity are superior to femaleness and femininity. However, trans women are targeted in specific ways (for example, as sexually adventurous and deceiving heterosexual men) that are different from the ways cisgender women are portrayed. Serano also points out that the discrimination trans women face is not simply transphobia, as evidenced by the fact that trans men are discriminated against but are not generally sexualized in the same ways as trans women.

Though many feminists today take an intersectional approach and support trans people's involvement in feminism, there remain small groups of trans-exclusionary radical feminists. Some of the most outspoken individuals have included Mary Daly, Sheila Jeffreys, Julie Bindel, and Germaine Greer. Their opposition to working with trans people is based on misunderstandings about what it means to be trans. One common argument made by anti-trans feminists is that trans people "reinforce the gender binary," therefore strengthening sexism. This is based on the false belief that all trans people are interested in transitioning to present as either ultra-masculine or ultra-feminine. Though such trans people exist, trans people, like cis people, fall all across the spectrum, and include butch dyke and tomboy trans women, as well as genderqueer people and trans men who are self-described "faggots." (See Myth 2, "All Trans People Want to Be Either Barbie or Ken.")

Because of their beliefs about trans people, anti-trans feminists sometimes attempt to limit trans participation in events using arguments that are based in gender essentialism and which contend that some issues and experiences are uniquely "male" or "female." Disregarding the notion that women "are made, not born," they claim that trans people cannot ever share in these and must forever remain excluded from being "true" men or women. Most commonly, anti-trans feminists exclude trans women from feminist gatherings, arguing that certain events should be "women only" and that trans women's inclusion is inappropriate and an expansion of male dominance into these spaces. Because trans women have not been socialized as women, they argue, they cannot understand cisgender women's oppression.

But in many ways the forms of discrimination faced by trans women are similar to those experienced by cis women. Murders of transgender women are commonplace, and harassment can be a daily occurrence.

Though most anti-trans feminist activism is directed toward trans women, trans men are also targeted. Specifically, some anti-trans feminists view trans men as "traitors" who, instead of transitioning, should have stayed living as women but as butch women. They argue that anyone can be masculine, whether male or female, and that transitioning to male is making a statement that in order to be masculine you have to be male. This often seems rooted in the idea that trans men are a betrayal of the butch identity, and again contradicts the notion of feminism as being a movement to expand sexual and gender autonomy.

Despite having very strong beliefs about trans identities, most anti-trans feminists likely have had little close social contact with trans people. Racist and homophobic views tend to diminish when people of different races and sexualities spend time together, and the same is probably true of transphobia. When people are seen as real, and no longer theoretical, it becomes harder to exclude them.

Today, though anti-trans feminists are vocal, they remain a small group. For the most part, feminists support trans people and see supporting transgender people as part of the feminist goal of breaking down gender barriers, and this is increasingly true with younger generations. Perhaps the most obvious incongruity in the myth that trans people and feminists don't get along is that, in fact, many feminists are transgender and many transgender people are feminists. Some trans feminists have even developed a unique brand of feminism called transfeminism, the initial creation of which is most often attributed to Emi Koyama. Transfeminism expands traditional feminist views about ownership over our bodies to include not only reproductive rights but also medical transition rights. Transfeminism also argues that every individual should be free to express their identity and have that identity respected.

The LGBTQ+ Community Is United

In 2007, Barney Frank, an openly gay man from Massachusetts, was serving in the United States House of Representatives. Along with a number of others, he introduced a bill—the Employment Non-Discrimination Act (ENDA)—that would protect against discrimination based on sexual orientation and gender identity. It wasn't the first time the legislation had been brought forward; since 1994, it had been introduced every year but one. However, 2007 was the first time the bill included gender identity.

Unfortunately, Frank's bill died in committee, and its proponents felt that they faced a choice: drop gender-identity protections or wait another year. Frank decided to introduce a new bill that did not include gender identity. Many LGBTQ+ organizations protested, but one of the largest and most well-funded—the Human Rights Campaign (HRC)—backed the new bill. Even after dropping trans protections, the bill passed the House but died in the Senate. Although Frank and others originally introduced a trans-inclusive ENDA, they were also the first to publicly backtrack on this inclusive vision. This led to a bitter divide between activists who felt that progress could only be made incrementally and those who believed that trans people's identities and needs were being ignored—that other parts of the queer community were willing to "throw trans-people under the bus."

For many trans people, the HRC/ENDA scandal represented more than a debate about one piece of legislation. It was also a reminder of multiple past betrayals. Since the founding of the gay rights movement, the role of transgender people has been precarious. On June 28, 1969, police conducted a raid of the Stonewall Inn in New York City's West Village. Instead of acquiescing as usual, customers fought back, leading to three nights of riots. For years, the Stonewall uprising was portrayed not only as the birth of the LGBTQ+ movement—writing out of history the work of homophile groups of the 1950s and early 1960s—but as the first revolt. Many accounts of the Stonewall riots focused on white gay men. Recent scholarship has revealed that Stonewall was preceded by similar instances of rebellion, including riots at Compton's Cafeteria in San Francisco and Cooper's Donuts in Los Angeles, both led by trans women of color. Historians have since corrected the record, documenting that many street youth, drag queens, and trans people (who called themselves transvestites at the time) were on the front lines during Stonewall.

Two of the most well-known trans figures in the early gay liberation movement were Sylvia Rivera and Marsha P. Johnson, the leaders of S.T.A.R., a group formed to help care for LGBTQ+ street youth. Johnson is said to have thrown the "shot glass heard around the world" that sparked the Stonewall riots, and Rivera to have launched the first Molotov cocktail (though she always insisted she had thrown the second). Rivera was a founding member of both the Gay Liberation Front and Gay Activists Alliance (GAA), and in photos both she and Johnson could be found out and proud leading demonstrations. During one protest, Rivera even scaled the wall of city hall. This in-your-face activism was extremely valuable to the movement, but at the same time often embarrassed more conservative activists. Many gay and lesbian activists did not want to be associated with gender nonconformity, preferring instead to present themselves to the public as exactly the same as straight people except in sexual attraction. Similar to the HRC/ENDA incident years later, advocates from the legal-reform-oriented GAA brought a nondiscrimination bill to the New York City Council but did not include protections for employees to dress as they wished.

Sadly, similar negative attitudes toward transgender people on the part of some mainstream gays and lesbians continue to exist today. During the 1990s and early 2000s, most large LGB organizations added a "T" to their names or official missions, although, for many, their policies did not reflect an investment in transgender issues. A 2015 Change.org petition called "Drop the T" made clear the differences of opinion that exist within LGBTQ+ organizations about transgender people. In an interview, the gay male author of the petition argued that

> gay/bisexual men and women just ARE—we don't need medicine or surgery to help us become who we believe we are, which is the case with the trans community. . . . The problem that develops when we are all under the same umbrella is that so many of our enemies see us as one and the same—that Caitlyn Jenner, for example, is a "homo," when that is not the case. . . . This is why I think the two groups should separate and fight for our respective rights on the more sure footing of our own ideas rather than conflating two divergent concepts.

Even those people and organizations who would never take such a public stance against trans inclusion often discriminate in more subtle ways. Many large national groups call themselves LGBT, for example, but are predominantly led by socioeconomically privileged white gays and lesbians, often primarily gay men. When trans people are invited to participate, they are often tokenized—their photos used to promote an image of diversity, while their opinions are discounted.

The causes that these large LGBTQ+ organizations take up also reflect their priorities. Much of the last two decades was spent strategizing around same-sex marriage rights, although some organizations did also devote significant resources to other issues such as employment discrimination, adoption and other family law issues, and HIV/AIDS work. A number of critics, including trans writers Dean Spade and Mattilda Bernstein Sycamore, have argued that fighting for a "piece of the pie" through marriage-equality initiatives reinforces the categories of haves and have-nots, and it does not center the experiences of the most marginalized within LGBTQ+ communities, including those who are poor, homeless, transgender, and people of color. Instead of pushing for marriage, critics argue, in order to gain health-care coverage for same-sex partners, we should be lobbying for nationalized health care, which would be more inclusive of the LGBTQ+ community as a whole.

The debates about the centrality of marriage equality are just the most recent in long-standing community discussions that reflect the distinct experiences of LGBTQ+ people based on their race, socioeconomic status, gender, and geography. For years, women have expressed their disappointment at the replication of patriarchy within organizations that emerged from these communities. "Dyke marches," which often occur during Pride Week in large cities, began in the early 1990s in response to the perceived invisibility of lesbians and disregard for lesbian issues within the larger, often male-oriented LGBTQ+ movement. Queers for Economic Justice (QEJ), a nonprofit active from 2002 to 2014, provided a strong critique of capitalism and of the corporatization of Pride, and made significant gains in improving conditions for LGBTQ+ people living in shelters.

QEJ and other organizations such as the Audre Lorde Project, run by LGBTQ+ people of color, have emphasized the intersecting oppressions faced by marginalized groups within LGBTQ+ communities, and in some instances, individual activists have challenged larger organizations to recognize these issues. In the wake of the

2015 police killing of a seventeen-year-old queer Latina woman, protestors stormed the stage at the Creating Change conference, one of the largest annual LGBTQ+ events in the country, sponsored by the National Gay and Lesbian Taskforce. They chanted "Trans Lives Matter!" and read a list of demands that emphasized the importance of movement organizations devoting more resources to trans and queer people of color.

Despite these fraught relationships within the LGBTQ+ community, there has been some progress in recent years. Blog posts proliferate about how gay, lesbian, and bisexual people can be good allies to their transgender friends and colleagues, demonstrating an interest on the part of many people to expand their knowledge. Trans people and LGBTQ+ people of color are occupying positions of increasing power within LGBTQ+ organizations, influencing the direction and type of activities they pursue. The LGBTQ+ community will never agree on everything, and it never should—diversity is one of its biggest assets. But hopefully, one day, it may be united in the pursuit of leaving no one behind.

ACKNOWLEDGMENTS

Together the authors would like to thank Gayatri Patnaik, editorial director at Beacon Press, for inviting us to be part of her important "myth-busting" series and Michael Bronski, series editor of Beacon's Queer Action/Queer Ideas series and author of *A Queer History of the United States*. We are grateful for their commitment to trans lives and for their detailed assistance with editing.

Laura Erickson-Schroth: Thanks so much to my parents for getting me off to a great start by putting me in baby t-shirts that said "I'm a Mini Feminist" and "Question Authority." And to my partner, Amanda—you always push me to think about things in new ways. I'm your #1 fan.

Laura A. Jacobs: To my friends, family, and other loved ones . . . to my teachers, advisors, mentors, and nemeses . . . to Lili Elbe, Christine Jorgensen, Renée Richards, Jamison Green, and many others . . . to Ray Bradbury, William Shakespeare, Kate Bush, and Stanley Kubrick . . . and special thanks to the Frances and Peter Jacobs Foundation for Their Wayward Children.

RESOURCES

MENTAL HEALTH CRISIS RESOURCES

Anti-Violence Project Hotline (212) 714–1141
This twenty-four-hour bilingual hotline offers assistance for LGBT survivors of violence.

Gay, Lesbian, Bisexual and Transgender (GLBT) National Hotline (888) 843-4564
The GLBT National Hotline provides telephone and online chat and e-mail peer-support, as well as factual information and local resources for cities and towns across the United States.

Trans Lifeline (877) 565–8860
Trans Lifeline runs a hotline staffed by transgender people for transgender people. Volunteers are ready to respond to whatever support needs members of our community might have.

Trevor Project (866) 488–7386
Founded in 1998 by the creators of the Academy Award–winning short film *Trevor*, the Trevor Project is the leading national organization providing crisis intervention and suicide prevention services to LGBTQ+ young people ages thirteen to twenty-four. In addition to a hotline, the Trevor Project offers options for youth to text and chat online with counselors.

FURTHER READING

Children/Teens

Arin Andrews. *Some Assembly Required: The Not-So-Secret Life of a Transgender Teen.* Simon & Schuster Books for Young Readers, 2015.

Cris Beam. *I Am J.* Little, Brown Books for Young Readers, 2012.

S. Bear Bergman and kd diamond. *Backwards Day.* Flamingo Rampant, 2012.

S. Bear Bergman and Suzy Malik. *The Adventures of Tulip, Birthday Wish Fairy*. Flamingo Rampant, 2012.

Colt Keo-Meier, Jesse Yang, Nine Lam Stacey. *Not a Girl*. Self-published, 2017.

Kirstin Cronn-Mills. *Beautiful Music for Ugly Children*. North Star Editions, 2012.

Tanita S. Davis. *Happy Families*. Ember, 2013.

Marcus Ewert. *10,000 Dresses*. Triangle Square, 2008.

Amy Fabrikant. *When Kayla Was Kyle*. Avid Readers, 2013.

Kim Fu. *For Today I Am a Boy*. Mariner Books, 2015.

Alex Gino. *George*. Scholastic Press, 2015.

Rachel Gold. *Being Emily*. Bella Books, 2012.

Katie Rain Hill. *Rethinking Normal: A Memoir in Transition*. Simon & Schuster Books for Young Readers, 2015.

Jazz Jennings. *Being Jazz: My Life as a (Transgender) Teen*. Crown Books for Young Readers, 2016.

Cheryl Kilodavis. *My Princess Boy*. Aladdin, 2010.

Susan Kulkin, ed. *Beyond Magenta: Transgender Teens Speak Out*. Candlewick, 2015.

David Levithan. *Every Day*. Ember, 2013.

Julie Anne Peters. *Luna*. Little, Brown Books for Young Readers, 2006.

Meredith Russo. *If I Was Your Girl*. Flatiron Books, 2016.

Rylan J. Testa and Deborah Coolhart. *The Gender Quest Workbook: A Guide for Teens and Young Adults Exploring Gender Identity*. Instant Help, 2015.

Ellen Wittlinger. *Parrotfish*. Simon & Schuster Books for Young Readers, 2007.

Jennie Wood. *A Boy Like Me*. 215 Ink, 2014.

Parents/Families/Professionals

Cris Beam. *Transparent: Love, Family, and Living the T with Transgender Teenagers*. Harvest Books, 2008.

Mary Boenke, ed. *Trans Forming Families: Real Stories About Transgendered Loved Ones*. 3rd ed. PFLAG Transgender Network, 2008.

Stephanie Brill. *The Transgender Child: A Handbook for Families and Professionals*. Cleis Press, 2008.

Stephanie Brill and Lisa Kenney. *The Transgender Teen: A Handbook for Parents and Professionals Supporting Transgender and Non-Binary Teens*. Cleis Press, 2016.

Diane Ehrensaft. *Gender Born, Gender Made: Raising Healthy Gender-Nonconforming Children*. 3rd revised ed. Experiment, 2011.

Diane Ehrensaft. *The Gender Creative Child: Pathways for Nurturing and Supporting Children Who Live Outside Gender Boxes*. Experiment, 2016.

Eleanor A. Hubbard and Cameron T. Whitley. *Trans-Kin: A Guide for Family and Friends of Transgender People*. Bolder Press, 2012.

Irwin Krieger, *Helping Your Transgender Teen: A Guide for Parents*. Genderwise Press, 2011.

Arlene Lev. *Transgender Emergence: Therapeutic Guidelines for Working with Gender-Variant People and Their Families*. Haworth Clinical Practice Press, 2004.

Elijah C. Nealy. *Transgender Children and Youth: Cultivating Pride and Joy with Families in Transition*. W. W. Norton & Company, 2017.

Amy Ellis Nutt. *Becoming Nicole: The Transformation of an American Family*. Random House, 2016.

Hillary Whittington. *Raising Ryland: Our Story of Parenting a Transgender Child with No Strings Attached*. William Morrow Paperbacks, 2016.

Fiction/Poetry

Ryka Aoki. *Seasonal Velocities: Poems, Stories, and Essays*. Trans-Genre Press, 2012.

Imogen Binnie. *Nevada, a Novel*. Topside Press, 2013.

Leslie Feinberg. *Stone Butch Blues*. Firebrand Books, 1993.

Roz Kaveney. *Dialectic of the Flesh*. A Midsummer Night's Press, 2012.

Roz Kaveney. *Tiny Pieces of Skull, or a Lesson in Manners*. Team Angelica Publishing, 2015.

Tom Leger and Riley MacLeod, eds. *The Collection: Short Fiction from the Transgender Vanguard*. Topside Press, 2012.

Sassafras Lowrey. *Lost Boi*. Arsenal Pulp Press, 2015.

Michael Scott Monje Jr. *Defiant*. Autonomous Press, 2015.

Shani Mootoo. *Moving Forward Sideways Like a Crab*. Doubleday Canada, 2014.

Casey Plett. *A Safe Girl to Love*. Topside Press, 2014.

Michael Quadland. *Offspring*. Red Hen Press, 2012.

Trish Salah. *Wanting in Arabic*. TSAR Publications, 2013.

K. M. Szpara, ed. *Transcendent: The Year's Best Transgender Speculative Fiction*. Lethe Press, 2016.

Nonfiction

S. Bear Bergman. *The Nearest Exit May Be Behind You*. Arsenal Pulp Press, 2010.

Peter Boag. *Re-Dressing America's Frontier Past*. University of California Press, 2012.

Kate Bornstein. *Gender Outlaw: On Men, Women, and the Rest of Us.* Vintage, 1994.

Kate Bornstein. *My New Gender Workbook: A Step-by-Step Guide to Achieving World Peace Through Gender Anarchy and Sex Positivity.* Routledge, 2013.

Patrick Califia. *Sex Changes: Transgender Politics.* Cleis Press, 2003.

Loren Cameron. *Body Alchemy: Transsexual Portraits.* Cleis Press, 1996.

Trystan Theosophus Cotten. *Hung Jury: Testimonies of Genital Surgery by Transsexual Men.* Transgender Press, 2012.

Noach Dzmura, ed. *Balancing on the Mechitza: Transgender in the Jewish Community.* Atlantic Books, 2010.

Dylan Edwards. *Transposes.* Northwest Press, 2012.

Anne Enke. *Transfeminist Perspectives in and beyond Transgender and Gender Studies.* Temple University Press, 2012.

Laura Erickson-Schroth, ed. *Trans Bodies, Trans Selves: A Resource for the Transgender Community.* Oxford University Press, 2014.

Anne Fausto-Sterling. *Myths of Gender: Biological Theories About Women and Men.* Basic Books, 1992.

Anne Fausto-Sterling. *Sex/Gender: Biology in a Social World.* Routledge, 2012.

Anne Fausto-Sterling. *Sexing the Body: Gender Politics and the Construction of Sexuality.* Basic Books, 2000.

Leslie Feinberg. *Transgender Warriors: Making History from Joan of Arc to Dennis Rodman.* Beacon Press, 1996.

Mel Reiff Hill and Jay Mays. *The Gender Book.* Marshall House Press, 2014.

Katrina Karkazis. *Fixing Sex: Intersex, Medical Authority, and Lived Experience.* Duke University Press, 2008.

Joanne Myerowitz. *How Sex Changed: A History of Transsexuality in the United States.* Harvard University Press, 2004.

Jay Prosser. *Second Skins: The Body Narratives of Transsexuality.* Columbia University Press, 1988.

Kristen Schilt. *Just One of the Guys? Transgender Men and the Persistence of Gender Inequality.* University of Chicago Press, 2011.

Julia Serano. *Excluded: Making Feminist and Queer Movements More Inclusive.* Seal Press, 2013.

Julia Serano. *Whipping Girl: A Transsexual Woman on Sexism and the Scapegoating of Femininity.* Seal Press, 2007.

Dean Spade. *Normal Life: Administrative Violence, Critical Trans Politics, and the Limits of Law.* South End Press, 2011.

Eric A. Stanley and Nat Smith, eds. *Captive Genders: Trans Embodiment and the Prison Industrial Complex.* AK Press, 2015.

Susan Stryker. *Transgender History.* Seal Press, 2008.

Susan Stryker and Stephen Whittle, eds. *The Transgender Studies Reader.* Routledge, 2006.

Rebecca Swan. *Assume Nothing.* Soft Skull Press, 2010.

Nicholas M. Teich. *Transgender 101: A Simple Guide to a Complex Issue.* Columbia University Press, 2012.

Michael Warner. *Fear of a Queer Planet: Queer Politics and Social Theory.* University of Minnesota Press, 1993.

Riki Anne Wilchins. *Queer Theory: An Instant Primer.* Alyson Books, 2004.

Riki Anne Wilchins. *Read My Lips: Sexual Subversion and the End of Gender.* Firebrand Books, 1997.

Memoir

Michelle Alexander and Michelle Diane Rose. *The Color of Sunlight: A True Story of Unconditional Acceptance Between a Rural RN and a Blind, Terminally-Ill Transsexual.* CreateSpace, 2010.

Alison Bechtel. *Fun Home: A Family Tragicomic.* Mariner Books, 2007.

S. Bear Bergman. *Blood, Marriage, Wine & Glitter.* Arsenal Pulp Press, 2013.

Justin Vivian Bond. *Tango: My Childhood, Backwards and in High Heels.* Feminist Press, 2011.

Helen Boyd. *She's Not the Man I Married: My Life with a Transgender Husband.* Seal Press, 2007.

Jennifer Finley Boylan. *She's Not There: A Life in Two Genders.* Broadway Books, 2013.

Jamison Green. *Becoming a Visible Man.* Vanderbilt University Press, 2004.

Matt Kailey. *Teeny Weenies and Other Short Subjects.* Outskirts Press, 2012.

Nick Krieger, *Nina Here Nor There: My Journey Beyond Gender.* Beacon Press, 2011.

Thomas Page McBee. *Man Alive: A True Story of Violence, Forgiveness and Becoming a Man.* City Lights/Sister Spit, 2014.

Janet Mock. *Redefining Realness: My Path to Womanhood, Identity, Love & So Much More.* Atria, 2014.

Beatriz Preciado. *Testo Junkie: Sex, Drugs, and Biopolitics in the Pharmacopornographic Era.* Feminist Press, 2013.

Megan M. Rohrer and Zander Keig, eds. *Letters for My Brothers: Transitional Wisdom in Retrospect.* Wilgefortis Press, 2014.

Daphne Scholinski. *The Last Time I Wore a Dress.* Riverhead Books, 1998.

Rae Spoon. *First Spring Grass Fire*. Arsenal Pulp Press, 2012.

Mattilda Bernstein Sycamore. *The End of San Francisco*. City Lights Publishers, 2013.

Zane Thimmesch-Gill. *Hiding in Plain Sight*. Riverdale Avenue Books, 2015.

Willy Wilkinson. *Born on the Edge of Race and Gender: A Voice for Cultural Competency*. Hapa Papa Press, 2015.

CONFERENCES

Black Trans Advocacy Conference

BTAC is a unique life-changing program that furthers education, provides linkage to resources, and offers community building and organizing, leadership development, and celebration of diverse identities. It includes a family day, pageant, ball, and awards gala. *http://www.blacktrans.org/conference*

Community Healthcare Network Annual Conference on Transgender Health

This conference features a keynote address, biomedical and behavioral tracks, and a series of breakout sessions covering transition-related care training for clinical providers. Some of the topics include surgical care, medical-legal issues, the social determinants of health, microaggressions, and other important subjects for primary medical care providers and specialists, social workers, public health professionals, community advocates, medical researchers, epidemiologists, and scientists. *http://www.chnnyc.org /6th-annual-conference-transgender-health*

Creating Change

The National LGBTQ Task Force sponsors and organizes this conference, one of the largest LGBTQ+ gatherings in the country. Since 1988, Creating Change has created opportunities for many thousands of committed people to develop and hone their skills, celebrate victories, build community, and be inspired by visionaries of our LGBTQ+ movement and allied movements for justice and equality. *http://www.creatingchange.org*

Fantasia Fair

Fantasia Fair is a week-long transgender event held every October in the LGBT resort town of Provincetown, Massachusetts. In 1975, the fair was conceived in response to a "need for cross-dressers and transsexuals to learn about themselves in an open, socially tolerant environment." Provincetown was picked as the host city because of its reputation for tolerance and as a gay and lesbian mecca. With some help from a couple of female impersonators who lived in town, some doctors practicing on Cape Cod, a few cosmetic consultants and about forty participants, Fantasia Fair went from an idea to reality. *http://www.fantasiafair.org*

Gender Conference East
Gender Conference East was established to bring together families and caregivers of all kinds; connect families and caregivers to one another as well as to providers and resources; create fun and safe spaces for children, tweens, and teens of all gender identities and expressions; welcome young adults, students, and professionals to learn from one another and deepen their understanding of gender; and welcome thought partners to keep us accountable as we learn year after year the practices that build and sustain inclusive schools, families, and communities. *http://www.genderconferenceeast.org*

Gender Odyssey
Gender Odyssey is an annual conference for families who are working to navigate the day-to-day realities of raising a gender diverse or transgender child. Gender Odyssey Family is an opportunity to find valuable resources, information and networking opportunities, and provides real tools to support and encourage your child's gender self-discovery. *http://www.gender odysseyfamily.org*

Gender Spectrum Family Conference and Professionals' Symposium
The Gender Spectrum Conference is an opportunity for youth and families to spend a weekend gaining the resources, information, and community needed to help young people effectively navigate their world. Workshops for caregivers, parents, and other family members focus on sharing information to help you support the children in your life. The symposium is ideal for professionals who work with gender-expansive youth and/or their families. Participants take part in programming, activities, and immediately accessible resources designed to build the capacity of professionals for working with families and young people around issues of gender. *https://www .genderspectrum.org*

GLMA: Health Professionals Advancing LGBT Equality
GLMA, formerly known as the Gay and Lesbian Medical Association, is an organization of health professionals working in LGBT health. GLMA's annual conference educates practitioners and students from across the health professions about the unique health needs of LGBT individuals

and families. The conference is a forum for discussion and exploration of how best to address these needs through research and clinical care. The conference also focuses on the needs of LGBT health professionals and health-profession students. *http://www.glma.org*

Philadelphia Trans Health Conference
PTHC was founded in 2001 and is the largest transgender-specific conference in the world, with more than two thousand attendees. Its mission is to educate and empower trans individuals on issues of health and well-being; educate and inform allies and health-service providers; and facilitate networking, community building, and systemic change. *https://www.mazzoni center.org/trans-health*

Southern Comfort Conference
Southern Comfort is a large conference that has taken place annually since 1991. It is attended by predominantly transgender women and pulls particularly from southern states, but it is also a welcoming space for people of all gender identities from a variety of geographic regions. There is an annual ball, a membership dinner, and local trips. *http://southerncomfortconference.org*

Translating Identity Conference
TIC explores a wide array of topics in discourses regarding gender and transgender identities, expressions, communities, and intersections. TIC is a free, student-organized, nonprofit conference that seeks to reach not only the University of Vermont and Burlington community but the nation as a whole. A one-day event, TIC has numerous sessions to choose from at any time that are directed toward people at all levels of inclusion in the trans and allied communities. *http://www.uvm.edu/translatingidentity*

World Professional Association for Transgender Health
Every two years, WPATH holds an international symposium focusing on the latest advances in research, education, clinical service, and advocacy to promote the health and well-being of transgender people and their families. *http://www.wpath.org*

FILMS

The Aggressives (dir. Daniel Peddle; 2005): A documentary look at the lives of six female-assigned people with a wide range of gender presentations who participate in New York City's predominantly African American drag balls.

Boy I Am (dir. Sam Feder and Julie Hollar; 2006): Though female-to-male transgender visibility has recently exploded in this country, conversations about trans issues in the lesbian community often run into resistance from the many queer women who view transitioning as a "trend" or as an anti-feminist act that taps into male privilege. *Boy I Am* is a feature-length documentary that begins to break down that barrier and promote dialogue about trans issues through a look at the experiences of three young transitioning FTMs in New York City—Nicco, Norie, and Keegan—as well as through the voices of lesbians, activists, and theorists who raise and address the questions many people have but few openly discuss.

Diagnosing Difference (dir. Annalise Ophelian; 2005): How does it feel to have your identity in the *Diagnostic and Statistical Manual of Mental Disorders*? This film interviews scholars, activists, and artists on the trans spectrum about the impact of the gender identity disorder (GID) diagnosis on their lives.

Free Cece! (dir. Jac Gares; 2016): On her way to the store with a group of friends, Chrishaun Reed "CeCe" McDonald was brutally attacked. While defending her life, a man was killed. After a coercive interrogation, CeCe was incarcerated in a men's prison in Minnesota. An international campaign to free CeCe garnered significant support from media and activists, including actress Laverne Cox. This film confronts the culture of violence surrounding trans women of color, and is told through the voices of Laverne Cox and Cece McDonald. *http://www.freececedocumentary.net/the -film.html*

Growing Old Gracefully: The Transgender Experience (dir. Joe Ippolito; 2014): For the first time in history, cohorts of trans and gender-nonconforming people are entering their senior years. This film showcases the personal experiences of three older trans people, as well as interviews with activists, clinicians, and researches. Additionally, the film looks at places where transphobia, ageism, racism, and classism intersect, and it explores the history of the trans movement. Some of the aging issues addressed in the film include health-care concerns, financial issues, housing problems, fear of loneliness, de-transitioning, and death and dying.

I'm Just Anneke (dir. Jonathan Skurnik, New Day Films; 2010): *I'm Just Anneke* is a portrait of a twelve-year-old girl who loves ice hockey and has a loving, close-knit family. Anneke is also a hardcore tomboy and everybody she meets assumes she's a boy. The onset of puberty has created an identity crisis for Anneke. Does she want to be a man or a woman when she grows up, or something in between? To give her more time to make a decision, her doctor has put her on Lupron, a hormone blocker that temporarily delays the hormones of adolescence. Despite rejection by her friends and struggles with suicidal depression, Anneke is determined to be true to herself and maintain a gender-fluid identity that matches what she feels on the inside. *I'm Just Anneke* takes us into the heart of a new generation of children who are intuitively questioning the binary-gender paradigm.

Kate Bornstein Is a Queer and Pleasant Danger (dir. Sam Feder; 2013): Performance artist and writer Kate Bornstein explodes binaries while deconstructing gender—and her own identity: Trans-dyke. Reluctant polyamorist. Sadomasochist. Recovering Scientologist. Pioneering gender outlaw. Sam Feder's playful and meditative portrait on Bornstein captures rollicking public performances and painful personal revelations as it bears witness to this trailblazing artist-theorist-activist who inhabits a space between male and female with wit, style, and astonishing candor.

Ma Vie En Rose (dir. Alain Berliner; 1997; French with English subtitles): In this film—the title of which translates to *My Life in Pink*—a young transgender child named Ludovic, raised as a boy, explores her gender as her parents and their new neighbors watch with confusion and anger. The other children in the film—one of whom is a child assigned female who prefers masculine clothing—help to highlight the role of play and exploration in identity development.

MAJOR! (dir. Annalise Ophelian; 2016): *MAJOR!* explores the life and campaigns of Miss Major Griffin-Gracy, a formerly incarcerated black transgender elder and activist who has been fighting for the rights of trans women of color for more than forty years. Miss Major is a veteran of the Stonewall rebellion, a survivor of Attica State Prison, and a former sex worker, but she is simply "Mama" to many in her community. Her personal story and activism for transgender civil rights highlight LGBT struggles for justice and equality from the 1960s to today. At the center of Griffin-Gracy's activism is her fierce advocacy for her girls, trans women of color who have survived police brutality and incarceration in men's jails and prisons.

Paris Is Burning (dir. Jennie Livingston; 1990): A chronicle of New York's LGBTQ+ scene in the 1980s, focusing on balls, voguing, and the ambitions and dreams of those who gave the era its warmth and vitality.

Screaming Queens: The Riot at Compton's Cafeteria (dir. Victor Silverman and Susan Stryker; 2005): A documentary about transgender women and drag queens who fought police harassment at Compton's Cafeteria in San Francisco's Tenderloin neighborhood in 1966, three years before the famous riots at the Stonewall Inn.

She's a Boy I Knew (dir. Gwen Haworth; 2007): Using interviews, animation, old family footage, and voice mail, Vancouver filmmaker Gwen Haworth documents her male-to-female gender transition partially through the voices of her anxious but loving family, best friend, and wife. The film focuses on the interpersonal relationships of a family who unexpectedly find their bonds strengthening as they overcome their preconceptions of gender and sexuality.

Southern Comfort (dir. Kate Davis; 2001): *Southern Comfort* documents the final year in the life of Robert Eads, a transgender man. Eads, diagnosed with ovarian cancer, was turned down for treatment by two dozen doctors out of their fear that treating such a patient would hurt their reputations. By the time Eads received treatment, the cancer was too advanced to save his life. However, he and his group of Southern transgender friends live on in this film.

Still Black: A Portrait of Black Transmen (2008): This film focuses on six black trans men and highlights the complex ways in which they navigate their lives, from learning to tie a tie to discussing the unique pressures they face as trans men of color. The cast members talk about their medical transitions, their sexual identities, their relationships with their fathers and brothers, and how they view masculinity.

Three to Infinity: Beyond Two Genders (dir. Lonny Shavelson; 2015). A documentary about people who are neither male nor female. Agender, genderqueer, and more, they're redefining gender, challenging masculinity and femininity, and taking us into a provocatively new gender frontier.

We've Been Around (dir. Rhys Ernst; 2016): Created by Rhys Ernst (coproducer of Amazon's hit *Transparent*) and produced by Christine Beebe, *We've Been Around* is a series of documentary shorts that chronicle the lives of transgender trailblazers. Episodes feature Lucy Hicks Anderson, Albert Cashier, Little Axe, and Lou Sullivan, as well as the organization Street Transvestite Action Revolutionaries and the movement Camp Trans. "Trans people have always existed, and have lived many different lives," Ernst said in a press release. "The central theme of *We've Been Around* is stated in the title. We've been here, throughout time, often hidden in plain sight. These stories show us just how important it is to share our histories."

FUNDING

The Astraea Lesbian Foundation for Justice
The Astraea Lesbian Foundation for Justice is the only philanthropic organization working exclusively to advance LGBTQ+ human rights around the globe. Astraea supports brilliant and brave grantee partners in the United States and internationally who challenge oppression and seed change. *http://www.astraeafoundation.org*

Jim Collins Foundation
The mission of the Jim Collins Foundation is to provide financial assistance to transgender people for gender-confirming surgeries. The foundation recognizes that not every transgender person needs or wants surgery to achieve a healthy transition. For those who do, gender-affirming surgeries are an important step in their transition to being their true selves. However, access to gender-affirming surgery is impossible for most. Discrimination against transgender people is so prevalent that many transgender people struggle to survive, never mind save for surgery costs. Even for those who have health insurance, coverage is systematically denied. *https://jimcollinsfoundation.org*

The Trans Justice Funding Project
The Trans Justice Funding Project is a community-led funding initiative, founded in 2012, to support grassroots, trans justice groups run by and for trans people. The project centers the leadership of trans people organizing around their experiences with racism, economic injustice, transmisogyny, ableism, immigration, incarceration, and other intersecting oppressions. Every penny raised goes to grantees with no restrictions and no strings attached. *http://www.transjusticefundingproject.org*

LEGAL

Lambda Legal
Founded in 1973, Lambda Legal is the oldest and largest national legal organization whose mission is to achieve full recognition of the civil rights of lesbians, gay men, bisexuals, transgender people, and those with HIV through impact litigation, education, and public-policy work. *http://www.lambdalegal.org*

GLAD

Through strategic litigation, public-policy advocacy, and education, GLBTQ Legal Advocates & Defenders works in New England and nationally to create a just society free of discrimination based on gender identity and expression, HIV status, and sexual orientation. *www.glad.org*

National Center for Lesbian Rights

Despite its name suggesting that NCLR works only on lesbian-related legal issues, this organization, founded in 1977, is committed to advancing the civil and human rights of LGBT people. NCLR litigates precedent-setting cases at the trial and appellate court levels, advocates for equitable public policies affecting the LGBT community, provides free legal assistance to LGBT people and their legal advocates, and conducts community education on LGBT issues. *http://www.nclrights.org*

The National Center for Transgender Equality

The National Center for Transgender Equality is a national social-justice organization devoted to ending discrimination and violence against transgender people through education and advocacy on issues of importance to transgender people. By empowering transgender people and allies to educate and influence policymakers and others, NCTE facilitates a strong and clear voice for transgender equality in our nation's capital and around the country. *http://www.transequality.org*

Sylvia Rivera Law Project

The Sylvia Rivera Law Project works to guarantee that all people are free to self-determine their gender identity and expression regardless of income or race and without facing harassment, discrimination, or violence. SRLP is a collective organization founded on the understanding that gender self-determination is inextricably intertwined with racial, social, and economic justice. Therefore, SRLP seeks to increase the political voice and visibility of low-income people and people of color who are transgender, intersex, or gender non-conforming. SRLP works to improve access to respectful and affirming social, health, and legal services for our communities. *http://srlp.org*

Transgender Law and Policy Institute

This nonprofit organization is dedicated to engaging in effective advocacy for transgender people in our society by bringing together experts and advocates to work on law and policy initiatives designed to advance transgender equality. The Transgender Law and Policy Institute makes weekly announcements of changes in state or federal law affecting trans people and hosts a searchable database on college and employer transgender policies and hate crime laws. *http://www.transgenderlaw.org*

Transgender Law Center

This organization works to change law, policy, and attitudes so that all people can live safely, authentically, and free from discrimination regardless of their gender identity or expression. The Transgender Law Center offers legal information and resources and hosts webinars as well as programs like its Detention Project, which works to end the abuses transgender and gender nonconforming people experience in prisons, jails, immigration detention, state hospitals, and other forms of detention, and at the hands of law enforcement. *http://transgenderlawcenter.org*

Transgender Legal Defense and Education Fund

TLDEF is committed to ending discrimination based upon gender identity and expression and to achieving equality for transgender people through public education, test-case litigation, direct legal services, community organizing and public-policy efforts. TLDEF continually seeks to leverage limited resources through innovative programs designed to harness the resources of the private bar for the public good. TLDEF's Name Change Project provides free, legal name-change services to community members through partnerships with some of nation's premier law firms and corporate law departments. *http://tldef.org*

OTHER ORGANIZATIONS

Ali Forney Center

Committed to saving the lives of LGBTQ+ youth, Carl Siciliano founded AFC in 2002 in memory of Ali, a gender-nonconforming teen who fled his home at thirteen, entered the foster-care system, and ended up living on the streets, where he was shot dead in 1997. AFC's mission is to protect LGBTQ+ youth from the harms of homelessness and empower them with the tools needed to live independently. Programs include a drop-in center, emergency and transitional housing, and medical and mental health care. *http://www.aliforneycenter.org*

Audre Lorde Project

ALP is a community-organizing center for lesbian, gay, bisexual, Two Spirit, trans, and gender-nonconforming (LGBTSTGNC) people of color communities. Initiated as an organizing effort by a coalition of LGBTSTGNC people of color, ALP was first brought together in 1994 by Advocates for Gay Men of Color, a multiracial network of gay men of color HIV policy advocates. The vision for ALP grew out of the expressed need for innovative and unified community strategies to address the multiple issues impacting LGBTSTGNC people of color communities. *http://alp.org*

Big Brothers Binder Program

This organization provides quality new or gently used binders to trans men eighteen and over (or younger when a parent makes contact) who would otherwise not be able to afford a new binder at retail prices due to hardship. Although controversial, the program is only for trans men who truly identify as male, wish to or are currently undergoing hormone replacement therapy, plan to have a double mastectomy with chest reconstruction, and plan to live or are currently living as male full time. *http://www.thetransitionalmale.com/BBUB.html*

Black and Pink

Black and Pink is an open family of LGBTQ+ prisoners and "free world" allies who support one another. Its work toward the abolition of the prison industrial complex is rooted in the experience of currently and formerly incarcerated people. Black and Pink is outraged by the specific violence of the prison industrial complex against LGBTQ+ people and responds through advocacy, education, direct service, and organizing. *http://www.blackandpink.org*

The Brown Boi Project

Launched in 2010, the Brown Boi Project works to build leadership, economic self-sufficiency, and the health of young masculine-of-center womyn, trans men, and queer/straight men of color, pipelining them into the social justice movement. The Brown Boi Project is a diverse and broad community, driven by a commitment to racial justice, gender justice, and transforming the privilege of masculinity into a tool for social change. The organization prioritizes support that improves the lives of masculine-of-center womyn and queer and trans people of color; works to transform the lives of women and girls; and introduces new alliances and tools for challenging racism, sexism, homophobia, and transphobia across our communities. *http://www.brownboiproject.org*

Camp Aranu'tiq Summer Camp

Camp Aranu'tiq is a week-long overnight summer camp for transgender and gender-variant youth ages eight to fifteen, with southern California and southern New England locations. The camp builds confidence, resilience, and community for transgender and gender-variant youth and their families. Aranu'tiq was founded in 2009 by Nick Teich, who dreamed of a safe and fun place for youth who felt they might not fit in at other camps because of their gender and/or who wanted to be with others like them. The first summer week in New England launched in 2010 with forty-one campers. Aranu'tiq also offers leadership programs for older teens and weekend family camps, and serves five hundred campers over the course of one year. *http://www.camparanutiq.org*

FIERCE!
FIERCE! is a membership-based organization building the leadership and power of LGBTQ+ youth of color in New York City. FIERCE! develops politically conscious leaders who are invested in improving themselves and their communities through youth-led campaigns, leadership development programs, and cultural expression through arts and media. FIERCE! is dedicated to cultivating the next generation of social justice movement leaders who are dedicated to ending all forms of oppression. *http://www.fiercenyc.org*

FORGE
FORGE is a national transgender antiviolence organization, founded in 1994. Since 2009, it has been federally funded to provide direct services to transgender, gender-nonconforming, and gender-nonbinary survivors of sexual assault. Since 2011, FORGE has served as the only transgender-focused organization federally funded to provide training and technical assistance to providers around the country who work with transgender survivors of sexual assault, domestic and dating violence, and stalking. *http://forge-forward.org*

Gender Creative Kids
The website GenderCreativeKids.ca provides resources for supporting and affirming gender-creative kids within their families, schools, and communities. By offering information and opportunities for connection between parents and caregivers, educators, health and social service providers, researchers, activists, and children/youth across Canada, Gender Creative Kids hopes to help transform the world into a safe, affirming, and joyful place for all children. GenderCreativeKids.ca is a joint effort between Gender Creative Kids Canada, a parent action group based in Montreal; Project 10, an LGBTQ+ youth organization based in Montreal; PFLAG Montreal, an

organization helping those who are struggling with issues of sexual orientation and gender identity; and the hosts of the National Workshop on Gender Creative Kids. *http://gendercreativekids.ca*

Gender Spectrum

Gender Spectrum's mission is to create a gender-inclusive world for all children and youth. To accomplish this, Gender Spectrum helps families, organizations, and institutions increase understandings of gender and consider the implications that evolving views have for each of us. *https://www .genderspectrum.org*

GLSEN

GLSEN (pronounced "glisten") was founded in 1990 by a small but dedicated group of Massachusetts schoolteachers who came together to improve an education system that too frequently allows its LGBTQ+ students to be bullied, discriminated against, or fall through the cracks. GLSEN provides resources for students and educators, including lesson plans, professional development, and support for Gay-Straight Alliances in schools. *http:// www.GLSEN.org*

The Hetrick-Martin Institute

The Hetrick-Martin Institute believes all young people, regardless of sexual orientation or identity, deserve a safe and supportive environment in which to achieve their full potential. Hetrick-Martin creates this environment for LGBTQ+ youth between the ages of thirteen and twenty-four and their families. Services include meals, clothing, high school equivalency preparation, job readiness, and counseling. *http://www.hmi.org*

LGBT Books to Prisoners

LGBT Books to Prisoners is a donation-funded, volunteer-run organization, based in Madison, Wisconsin, that sends books and other educational materials free of charge to LGBTQ-identified prisoners across the United States. LGBT Books to Prisoners has been in operation for nearly ten years and has sent books to more than six thousand prisoners in that time; in 2015, 3,042 packages of books were sent. *https://lgbtbookstoprisoners.org*

The National LGBT Cancer Network

The National LGBT Cancer Network works to improve the lives of LGBT cancer survivors and those at risk by educating the LGBT community about our increased cancer risks and the importance of screening and early detection; training health-care providers to offer more culturally competent, safe, and welcoming care; and advocating for LGBT survivors in mainstream cancer organizations, the media, and research. *http://www.cancer-network.org*

The National Resource Center on LGBT Aging

The National Resource Center on LGBT Aging is the country's first and only technical-assistance resource center aimed at improving the quality of services and supports offered to LGBT older adults. Established in 2010 through a federal grant from the US Department of Health and Human Services, the National Resource Center on LGBT Aging offers training, technical assistance, and educational resources to providers, LGBT organizations, and LGBT older adults. The center is led by Services & Advocacy for GLBT Elders (SAGE) in collaboration with eighteen leading organizations from around the country. *http://www.lgbtagingcenter.org*

PFLAG

Founded in 1972 with the simple act of a mother publicly supporting her gay son, PFLAG is the nation's largest family and ally organization. Uniting people who are LGBTQ+ with families, friends, and allies, PFLAG is committed to advancing equality through its mission of support, education, and advocacy. PFLAG has four hundred chapters and two hundred thousand supporters crossing multiple generations of American families in major urban centers, small cities, and rural areas in all fifty states, the District of Columbia, and Puerto Rico. *https://www.pflag.org*

Project Health

Lyon-Martin Health Services, founded in 1979 as a clinic for lesbians, hosts Project Health, a national transgender medical service that provides presentations on transgender health care, rotations for health professions students, support for clinics interested in providing transgender health care, and a national online transgender medical consultation service (Transline) for health care providers. *http://project-health.org*

Safe Schools Coalition

Safe Schools Coalition, located in Washington State, is a public-private partnership in support of gay, lesbian, bisexual, transgender, queer, and questioning youth that works to help schools become safe places where every family can belong, every educator can teach, and every child can learn, regardless of gender, gender identity, or sexual orientation. *http://www .safeschoolscoalition.org*

Services & Advocacy for GLBT Elders (SAGE)

Services & Advocacy for GLBT Elders is the country's largest and oldest organization dedicated to improving the lives of LGBT older adults and their caregivers. Founded in 1978 and headquartered in New York City, SAGE offers supportive services and consumer resources, advocates for public-policy changes to address the needs of LGBT older people, and provides training for providers and LGBT organizations, largely through its National Resource Center on LGBT Aging. With offices in New York City, Washington, DC, and Chicago, SAGE coordinates a growing network of thirty local SAGE affiliates in twenty states and the District of Columbia. *http://www.sageusa.org*

TGI Justice Project

The TGI Justice Project is a group of transgender, gender-variant and intersex people—inside and outside prisons, jails, and detention centers—creating a united family in the struggle for survival and freedom. TGI Justice works in collaboration with others to forge a culture of resistance and resilience to strengthen us for the fight against human rights abuses, imprisonment, police violence, racism, poverty, and societal pressures. TGI Justice seeks to create a world rooted in self-determination, freedom of expression, and gender justice. *http://www.tgijp.org*

TransActive Gender Center

An internationally recognized nonprofit focused on serving the diverse needs of transgender and gender-nonconforming children, youth, and their families and allies, the TransActive Gender Center provides a holistic range of services and expertise to empower transgender and gender-diverse children, youth, and their families in living healthy lives, free of discrimination. *http://www.transactiveonline.org*

TransAthlete

TransAthlete.com is a resource for students, athletes, coaches, and administrators to find information about trans inclusion in athletics at various levels of play. *www.transathlete.com*

Transgender Archives

The Transgender Archives at the University of Victoria, Canada, is committed to the preservation of the history of pioneering activists, community leaders, and researchers who have contributed to the betterment of transgender and gender-nonconforming people. Since 2007, the Transgender Archives has been actively acquiring documents, rare publications, and memorabilia of persons and organizations associated with activism by and for transgender and gender-nonconforming people. The Transgender Archives began with the generous donation of the Rikki Swin Institute collection and has been enhanced by other significant donations, including the personal papers of Reed Erickson, the entire University of Ulster Trans-Gender Archive collection, and the records of Zenith Foundation of Vancouver Canada, among many others. The Transgender Archives' records of research related to trans and gender-nonconforming people go back over one hundred years, while records of activism by trans and gender-nonconforming people span more than fifty years and come from eighteen countries across five continents. The collections comprise the largest trans archives in the world. *http://www.uvic.ca/transgenderarchives*

Transgender Oral History Project

The Transgender Oral History Project is a community-driven effort to collect and share a diverse range of stories from within transgender and gender-variant communities promoting grassroots media projects, documenting trans people's experiences, maintaining a publicly accessible digital archive, and teaching media production skills. *http://transoralhistory.com*

TransParent

TransParent envisions a world that honors and affirms the natural human experience of gender independence. TransParent's mission is to normalize this experience by supporting and encouraging parents to act in their child's best interest; empowering gender independent children to live authentically; identifying and organizing experienced and knowledgeable local resources to assist families; and creating safe spaces in our community for gender-independent children. *http://www.transparentsUSA.org*

Trans Kids Purple Rainbow

Trans Kids Purple Rainbow is committed to the premise that gender dysphoria is something a child can't control and it is society that needs to change, not the child. Families need to support their children and be encouraged to allow them to grow-up free of gender roles. *http://www.transkidspurple rainbow.org/about-us*

Trans People of Color Coalition

Founded in 2010, Trans People of Color Coalition was created by people of color who felt unheard and underrepresented in the trans equality movement. TPOCC became an effort to organize trans people of color to fill the void of representation of POC voices included in making key decisions that impact the trans community at large. *http://transpoc.org*

The Trans Youth Equality Foundation

The Trans Youth Equality Foundation provides education, advocacy, and support for transgender and gender-nonconforming youth and their families. The foundation's mission is to share information about the unique needs of this community, partnering with families, educators, and service providers to help foster a healthy, caring, and safe environment for all transgender children. *http://www.transyouthequality.org*

NOTES

MYTH 1: YOU'VE NEVER MET A TRANSGENDER PERSON

Kerith J. Conron, Gunner Scott, Grace Sterling Stowell, and Stewart J.
Landers, "Transgender Health in Massachusetts: Results from a
Household Probability Sample of Adults," *American Journal of Public
Health* 102, no. 1 (2012): 118–22.

Lynn Conway, "How Frequently Does Transsexualism Occur?," University
of Michigan, 2012, http://ai.eecs.umich.edu/people/conway/TS
/TSprevalence.html.

Gary J. Gates, "How Many People Are Lesbian, Gay, Bisexual, and Transgender?," Williams Institute, 2011, http://williamsinstitute.law.ucla.edu
/wp-content/uploads/Gates-How-Many-People-LGBT-Apr-2011.pdf.

MYTH 2: ALL TRANS PEOPLE WANT TO BE EITHER BARBIE OR KEN

Rachel Abrams, "Barbie Adds Curvy and Tall to Body Shapes," *New York
Times*, January 28, 2016, http://www.nytimes.com/2016/01/29/business
/barbie-now-in-more-shapes.html.

Genny Beemyn, "US History," in *Trans Bodies, Trans Selves: A Resource for
the Transgender Community*, ed. Laura Erickson-Schroth (New York:
Oxford University Press, 2014).

Harry Benjamin, *The Transsexual Phenomenon* (New York: Julian Press,
1966).

H. Dittmar, E. Halliwell, and S. Ive, "Do Barbie Dolls Make Girls Want to
Be Thin?," *Developmental Psychology* 42, no. 2 (2006): 283–92.

Erica Rand, *Barbie's Queer Accessories* (Durham: Duke University Press, 1995).

Eli Coleman et al., "Standards of Care for the Health of Transsexual, Transgender, and Gender-Nonconforming People, Version 7," *International
Journal of Transgenderism* 13, no. 4 (2012): 165–232.

MYTH 3: YOU'RE NOT REALLY TRANS IF YOU HAVEN'T HAD "THE SURGERY"

Jules Chyten-Brennan, "Surgical Transition," in Erickson-Schroth, *Trans Bodies, Trans Selves.*

Coleman et al., "Standards of Care for the Health of Transsexual, Transgender, and Gender-Nonconforming People, Version 7."

Laura Erickson-Schroth, Marci L. Bowers, and Tamar C. Carmel, "Transgender Surgery," in *The International Encyclopedia of Human Sexuality*, 3 vols., ed. Patricia Whelehan and Anne Bolin (Chichester, West Sussex, UK: Wiley-Blackwell, 2015).

MYTH 4: TRANS PEOPLE ARE "TRAPPED IN THE WRONG BODY"

Benjamin, *The Transsexual Phenomenon.*

Laura Erickson-Schroth, "Update on the Biology of Transgender Identity," *Journal of Gay & Lesbian Mental Health* 17, no. 2 (2013): 150–74.

Laura Erickson-Schroth, Miqqi Alicia Gilbert, and T. Evan Smith, "Sex and Gender Development," in Erickson-Schroth, *Trans Bodies, Trans Selves.*

Anne Fausto-Sterling, *Myths of Gender: Biological Theories of Women and Men* (New York: Basic Books, 1992).

———, *Sexing the Body: Gender Politics and the Construction of Sexuality* (New York: Basic Books, 2000).

———, *Sex/Gender: Biology in a Social World* (New York: Routledge, 2012).

Rebecca M. Jordan-Young, *Brain Storm: The Flaws in the Science of Sex Differences* (Cambridge, MA: Harvard University Press, 2010).

Francine Russo, "Is There Something Unique About the Transgender Brain?," *Scientific American*, January 1, 2016, https://www.scientific american.com/article/is-there-something-unique-about-the -transgender-brain/.

MYTH 5: TRANS PEOPLE ARE SECRETLY GAY

Tim Bergling, *Sissyphobia: Gay Men and Effeminate Behavior* (New York: Southern Tier Editions, 2001).

Shinsuke Eguchi, "Negotiating Hegemonic Masculinity: The Rhetorical Strategy of 'Straight-Acting' Among Gay Men," *Journal of Intercultural Communication Research* 38, no. 3 (2009): 193–209.

Sabra L. Katz-Wise et al., "Differences in Sexual Orientation Diversity and Sexual Fluidity in Attractions Among Gender Minority Adults in Massachusetts," *Journal of Sex Research* 53, no. 1 (2016): 74–84.

Andrea L. Roberts et al., "Childhood Gender Nonconformity: A Risk Indicator for Childhood Abuse and Posttraumatic Stress in Youth," *Pediatrics* 129, no. 3 (2012): 410–17.

Andrea L. Roberts et al., "Childhood Gender Nonconformity, Bullying Victimization, and Depressive Symptoms Across Adolescence and Early Adulthood: An 11-Year Longitudinal Study," *Journal of the American Academy of Child and Adolescent Psychiatry* 52, no. 2 (2013): 143–52.

W. Christopher Skidmore et al., "Gender Nonconformity and Psychological Distress in Lesbians and Gay Men," *Archives of Sexual Behavior* 35, no. 6 (2006): 685–97.

Kittiwut Jod Taywaditep, "Marginalization Among the Marginalized: Gay Men's Anti-Effeminacy Attitudes," *Journal of Homosexuality* 42, no. 1 (2002): 1–28.

MYTH 6: IT'S RUDE TO ASK HOW YOU SHOULD ADDRESS SOMEONE

Jessica Bennett, "She? Ze? They? What's in a Gender Pronoun?," *New York Times*, January 30, 2016, http://www.nytimes.com/2016/01/31/fashion /pronoun-confusion-sexual-fluidity.html.

Jennifer Conlin, "The Freedom to Choose Your Pronoun," *New York Times*, September 30, 2011, http://www.nytimes.com/2011/10/02/fashion /choosing-a-pronoun-he-she-or-other-after-curfew.html?_r=0.

Gender Neutral Pronoun Blog, https://genderneutralpronoun.wordpress .com/.

Tamara Khandaker, "U of T Prof Ignores University's Demands He Use Students' Preferred Gender Pronouns," *VICE*, October 20, 2016, http:// www.vice.com/en_ca/read/u-of-t-prof-ignores-universitys-demand -he-use-students-preferred-gender-pronouns.

Elizabeth Reis, "Pronoun Privilege," *New York Times*, September 25, 2016, http://www.nytimes.com/2016/09/26/opinion/pronoun-privilege .html?_r=0.

Todd Starnes, "'His Majesty': Student Single-Handedly Defeats an Army of Gender Neutral Activists," Fox News Opinion, September 30, 2016, http://www.foxnews.com/opinion/2016/09/30/his-majesty-student -single-handedly-defeats-army-gender-neutral-activists.html.

Kate Steinmetz, "This Gender-Neutral Word Could Replace 'Mr.' and 'Ms.,'" *Time*, November 10, 2015, http://time.com/4106718/what -mx-means/.

Alex Williams, "Is Hayden a Boy or Girl? Both. 'Post-Gender' Baby Names Are on the Rise," *New York Times*, August 18, 2016, http:// www.nytimes.com/2016/08/21/fashion/gender-neutral-baby -names.html.

Hannah Cregan Zigler, "Transgender Actress Laverne Cox Delivers Speech in Marshall Auditorium," *Clerk*, November 10, 2014,

http://haverfordclerk.com/transgender-actress-laverne-cox-delivers
-speech-in-marshall-auditorium/.

MYTH 7: "SURE, I'D LOVE TO TALK ABOUT WHAT'S IN MY PANTS"

Loren Cameron, *Body Alchemy: Transsexual Portraits* (Pittsburgh: Cleis
Press, 1996).

Katie McDonough, "Laverne Cox Flawlessly Shuts Down Katie Couric's
Invasive Questions About Transgender People," *Salon*, January 7, 2014,
http://www.salon.com/2014/01/07/laverne_cox_artfully_shuts_down
_katie_courics_invasive_questions_about_transgender_people/.

Christine Jorgensen, *Christine Jorgensen: A Personal Autobiography* (New
York: Bantam Books, 1968).

MYTH 8: MOST TRANS PEOPLE ARE SEX WORKERS AND HAVE HIV

Augustus Klein and Sarit A. Golub, "Family Rejection as a Predictor of Suicide Attempts and Substance Misuse Among Transgender and Gender
Nonconforming Adults," *LGBT Health* 3, no. 3 (June 2016): 193–99.

Erin Fitzgerald et al., *Meaningful Work: Transgender Experiences in the Sex
Trade* (Trans Equality, December 2015), http://www.transequality
.org/sites/default/files/Meaningful%20Work-Full%20Report_FINAL
_3.pdf.

Karen I. Fredriksen-Goldsen et al., *The Aging and Health Report: Disparities
and Resilience Among Lesbian, Gay, Bisexual, and Transgender Older Adults*
(Seattle: Institute for Multigenerational Health, 2011), http://caringand
aging.org/wordpress/wp-content/uploads/2011/05/Full-Report-FINAL
-11-16-11.pdf.

Jaime M. Grant et al., *Injustice at Every Turn: A Report of the National
Transgender Discrimination Survey* (Washington, DC: National Gay and
Lesbian Task Force/National Center for Transgender Equality, 2011),
http://www.transequality.org/sites/default/files/docs/resources/
NTDS_Report.pdf.

Mike Mariani, "Exchanging Sex for Survival," *Atlantic*, June 26, 2014,
http://www.theatlantic.com/health/archive/2014/06/exchanging-sex
-for-survival/371822/.

Asher Moses, "Our Sexual Desires Exposed by Neuroscientists' Porn
Study," *Sydney Morning Herald*, June 21, 2011, http://www.smh.com
.au/technology/technology-news/our-sexual-desires-exposed-by
-neuroscientists-porn-study-20110621-1gcol.html.

Larry Nuttbrock et al., "Lifetime Risk Factors for HIV/STI Infections Among Male-to-Female Transgender Persons," *Journal of Acquired Immune Deficiency Syndrome* 52, no. 3 (November 1, 2009): 417–21.

Red Umbrella Project, http://www.redumbrellaproject.org.

Stefan Rowniak et al., "Transmen: The HIV Risk of Gay Identity," *AIDS Education and Prevention* 23, no. 6 (2011): 508, http://www.hivplusmag.com/case-studies/2013/04/08/invisible-women-why-transgender-women-are-hit-so-hard-hiv.

Sex Workers Project, http://sexworkersproject.org.

Sex Workers' Rights Advocacy Network (SWAN), http://swannet.org.

Carrie Weisman, "Why Trans Porn Is Hugely Popular Among Hetero Men," *Alternet*, June 6, 2016, http://www.alternet.org/sex-amp-relationships/why-trans-porn-hugely-popular-among-hetero-men.

MYTH 9: TRANS PEOPLE HATE THEIR BODIES

Michael Aaron, "BDSM as Harm Reduction," *Standard Deviations*, blog, *Psychology Today*, October 13, 2016, https://www.psychologytoday.com/blog/standard-deviations/201610/bdsm-harm-reduction.

Michael Aaron, "Enough with the Trauma," *Standard Deviations*, blog, *Psychology Today*, August 3, 2016, https://www.psychologytoday.com/blog/standard-deviations/201608/enough-the-trauma-reductionism.

Carolin Klein and Boris B. Gorzalka, "Continuing Medical Education: Sexual Functioning in Transsexuals Following Hormone Therapy and Genital Surgery: A Review (CME)," *Journal of Sexual Medicine* 6, no. 11 (2009): 2922–39.

Alexis D. Light et al., "Transgender Men Who Experienced Pregnancy After Female-to-Male Gender Transitioning," *Obstetrics & Gynecology* 124, no. 6 (2014): 1120–27.

S. M. Peitzmeier et al., "Pap Test Use Is Lower Among Female-to-Male Patients Than Non-Transgender Women," *American Journal of Preventive Medicine* 47, no. 6 (2014): 808–12, http://doi.org/10.1016/j.amepre.2014.07.031.

The Philadelphia Center for Transgender Surgery, "Frequently Asked Questions," http://www.thetransgendercenter.com/index.php?option=com_content&view=article&id=75&Itemid=145.

S. L. Reisner et al., "Legal Protections in Public Accommodations Settings: A Critical Public Health Issue for Transgender and Gender-Nonconforming People," *Milbank Quarterly* 93, no. 3 (2015): 484–515.

G. Selvaggi et al., "Genital Sensitivity After Sex Reassignment Surgery in Transsexual Patients," *Annals of Plastic Surgery* 58, no. 4 (April 2007): 427–33, https://www.ncbi.nlm.nih.gov/pubmed/17413887.

Kai Cheng Thom, "How Trans Women Are Reclaiming Their Orgasms," *Buzzfeed LGBT*, April 17, 2016, https://www.buzzfeed.com/kaichengthom /the-search-for-trans-womens-orgasms?utm_term=.xkLyMbxox# .csWQGordr.

MYTH 10: TRANS PEOPLE ARE TRYING TO TRICK OTHERS

Carsten Balzer, *Every 3rd Day the Murder of a Trans Person Is Reported* (Liminalis, July 2009), http://www.liminalis.de/2009_03/TMM/tmm -englisch/Liminalis-2009-TMM-report2008-2009-en.pdf.

Sarah E. Belawski and Carey Jean Sojka, "Intimate Relationships," in Erickson-Schroth, *Trans Bodies, Trans Selves*.

Shayna Jacobs, "Murder Suspect Said His 'Manhood' Was Threatened When He Found Out He Was Hitting on Transgender Woman," *New York Daily News*, April 1, 2016, http://www.nydailynews.com/new-york/nyc -crime/transgender-slay-suspect-manhood-threatened-article -1.2585915.

Cynthia Lee and Peter Kar Yu Kwan, "The Trans Panic Defense: Heteronormativity, and the Murder of Transgender Women," 66 *Hastings Law Journal* 77 (2014), GWU Law School Public Law Research Paper No. 2014-10, http://scholarship.law.gwu.edu/cgi/viewcontent.cgi?article =2377&context=faculty_publications.

Paris Lees, "Should Trans People Have to Disclose Their Birth Gender Before Sex?," *Vice*, July 1, 2013, http://www.vice.com/read/should -trans-people-have-to-disclose-their-birth-gender-before-sex.

Parker Marie Molloy, "California Becomes First State to Ban Gay, Trans 'Panic' Defenses," *Advocate*, September 29, 2014, http://www .advocate.com/crime/2014/09/29/california-becomes-first-state -ban-gay-trans-panic-defenses.

Rebecca Rosenberg, "Man Cops Plea in Transgender Woman's Fatal Beating," *New York Post*, April 4, 2016, http://nypost.com/2016/04/04 /man-who-killed-transgender-woman-in-blind-fury-takes -plea-deal/.

"Should It Be Illegal for a Transsexual to Trick a Straight Person?," Debate .org, http://www.debate.org/opinions/should-it-be-illegal-for-a -transsexual-to-trick-a-straight-person, accessed January 10, 2017.

Reid Vanderburgh, "Coming Out," in Erickson-Schroth, *Trans Bodies, Trans Selves*.

MYTH 11: MOST TRANS PEOPLE CAN'T FIND PARTNERS AND END UP LONELY

Erving Goffman, *Stigma: Notes on the Management of Spoiled Identity* (New York: Simon & Schuster, 1963).

Lewis Hancox, "12 Things You Should Know Before Dating a Transgender Guy," *Cosmopolitan*, December 23, 2015, http://www.cosmopolitan.co.uk/love-sex/relationships/a40338/dating-transgender-guy-information/.

Jazz Jennings, "15-Year-Old Transgender Girl Opens Up About Her Quest to Find Love," *Harper's Bazaar*, October 18, 2016, http://www.harpersbazaar.com/culture/features/a17833/women-who-dare-jazz-jennings/.

Megan, "A Beginner's Guide to Dating a Transgendered Person," *Perks Magazine*, October 17, 2013, http://perksmag.com/sexuality/beginners-guide-dating-transgendered-person/.

Jay McNeil et al., *Trans Mental Health Study 2012* (Scottish Transgender Alliance, September 2012), http://www.scottishtrans.org/wp-content/uploads/2013/03/trans_mh_study.pdf.

Singles in America, survey, Match.com, 2015, http://www.singlesinamerica.com.

Kai Cheng Thom, "6 Things Every Man Who Dates Trans Women Needs to Know," *Everyday Feminism*, October 7, 2015, http://everydayfeminism.com/2015/10/men-who-date-trans-women/.

MYTH 12: TRANS PEOPLE ARE A DANGER TO OTHERS, ESPECIALLY CHILDREN

Advocates for Youth, *Tips and Strategies for Addressing the Challenges That Face Transgender Youth*, http://www.advocatesforyouth.org/publications/publications-a-z/497-tips-and-strategies-for-addressing-the-challenges-that-face-transgender-youth, accessed December 19, 2016. Document adapted with permission from the Transgender Law Center, *Transgender and Gender Non-Conforming Youth: Recommendations for Schools* (San Francisco: The Center, 2003).

Anti-Violence Project, "Hate Violence Against Transgender Communities," http://www.avp.org/storage/documents/ncavp_transhvfactsheet.pdf, accessed December 19, 2016.

Marcie Blanco, "Statistics Show Exactly How Many Times Trans People Have Attacked You in Bathrooms," Mic.com, April 2, 2015, https://mic.com/articles/114066/statistics-show-exactly-how-many-times-trans-people-have-attacked-you-in-bathrooms#.yyn2vBnyG .

Leslie Cooper, *Protecting the Rights of Transgender Parents and Their Children: A Guide for Parents and Lawyers* (New York: ACLU, March 2013), https://www.aclu.org/files/assets/aclu-tg_parenting_guide.pdf.

John Cotter, "Transgender Teacher's Complaint to Be Heard," *Global News*, January 12, 2014, http://globalnews.ca/news/1075170/transgender-teachers-complaint-to-be-heard/.

Mara Gay, "City Seeking to Diversify Foster Care System," *Wall Street Journal*, June 2, 2013, http://www.wsj.com/articles/SB10001424127887324563004578521604208702758.

Emanuela Grinberg, "Settlement Reached in Transsexual Custody Case," CNN International, June 16, 2005, http://edition.cnn.com/2005/LAW/06/16/ctv.transsexual.custody/.

Klein and Golub, "Family Rejection as a Predictor of Suicide Attempts and Substance Misuse Among Transgender and Gender Nonconforming Adults."

Slav Kornik, "Alberta Catholic School District Spent $367,000 on Legal Battle with Transgender Teacher," *Global News*, May 2, 2016, http://globalnews.ca/news/2674951/alberta-catholic-school-district-spent-367000-on-legal-battle-with-transgender-teacher/.

Ines San Martin, "Pope Calls Gender Theory a 'Global War' Against the Family," *Crux*, October 1, 2016, https://cruxnow.com/global-church/2016/10/01/pope-calls-gender-theory-global-war-family/.

Janet Mock, "Trans Women *Are* Real Women: Janet Mock on How Her Role Models Shaped Her Journey," *Marie Claire*, April 23, 2015, http://www.marieclaire.com/beauty/news/a14161/my-transgender-beauty-role-models/.

National Alliance on Mental Illness, "LGBTQ," https://www.nami.org/Find-Support/LGBTQ, accessed December 19, 2016.

Kristina R. Olson et al., "Mental Health of Transgender Children Who Are Supported in Their Identities," *Pediatrics* (February 2016), peds.2015-3223; DOI: 10.1542/peds.2015-3223.

Monica Roberts, "Why Black Transgender Role Models Are Important," *TransGriot*, April 19, 2009, http://transgriot.blogspot.com/2009/04/why-black-transgender-role-models-are.html.

Sam Roberts, "Marla Krolikowski, Transgender Teacher Fired for Insubordination, Dies at 62," *New York Times*, September 28, 2015, http://www.nytimes.com/2015/09/28/nyregion/marla-krolikowski-transgender-teacher-fired-for-insubordination-dies-at-62.html?_r=0.

Rebecca L. Stotzer, Jody L. Herman, and Amira Hasenbush, *Transgender Parenting: A Review of Existing Research* (Los Angeles: Williams Institute, UCLA Law School, October 2014).

Danielle Tcholkian, "Students Fight for Teacher Allegedly Fired for Being Transgender," *Metro*, December 9, 2014, http://www.metro.us/local

/students-fight-for-teacher-allegedly-fired-for-being-transgender
/tmWman---8b4TZrkPRHoA/.

MYTH 13: "YOU'RE IN THE WRONG BATHROOM!"

Travis M. Andrews, "Target CEO Responds to Nationwide Boycott of the
Store Over Transgender Bathroom Policy," *Washington Post*, May 13,
2016, https://www.washingtonpost.com/news/morning-mix/wp/2016
/05/13/target-ceo-responds-to-nationwide-boycott-of-the-store
-over-transgender-bathroom-policy/.

Jake Damien, "As a Transgender Man, Choosing Which Bathroom to Use
Can Be Agony," *Fusion*, June 28, 2016, http://fusion.net/story/320068
/transgender-man-bathrooms-locker-rooms-fear/.

Jody L. Herman, "Gendered Restrooms and Minority Stress: The Public
Regulation of Gender and Its Impact on Transgender People's Lives,"
Journal of Public Management & Social Policy (Spring 2013), http://
williamsinstitute.law.ucla.edu/wp-content/uploads/Herman-Gendered
-Restrooms-and-Minority-Stress-June-2013.pdf.

Human Rights Watch, *Shut Out: Restrictions on Bathroom and Locker Room
Access for Transgender Youth in US Schools* (New York: Human Rights
Watch, September 13, 2016), https://www.hrw.org/report/2016/09/13
/shut-out/restrictions-bathroom-and-locker-room-access-transgender
-youth-us-schools.

Mitch Kellaway, "Woman Sues Restaurant That Ejected Her from the Bathroom for Looking 'Like a Man,'" *Advocate*, June 17, 2015, http://www
.advocate.com/business/2015/06/17/detroit-woman-kicked-out
-restaurant-bathroom-looking-man-sues.

Jennifer 8 Lee, "Ejection of a Woman from a Women's Room Prompts Lawsuit," *New York Times*, October 9, 2007, http://cityroom.blogs.nytimes
.com/2007/10/09/ejection-of-a-woman-from-a-womens-room
-prompts-lawsuit/.

Joe Morgan, "Trans Man Takes on Selfie Campaign to Fight 'Ridiculous'
Bathroom Bans," *Gay Star News*, March 12, 2015, http://www.gaystar
news.com/article/trans-man-takes-selfie-campaign-fight-ridiculous
-bathroom-bans120315/#gs.iHpdlOc.

JamesMichael Nichols, "Trans Woman Asks: 'You Really Want Me in the
Same Bathroom as Your Husband?,'" *Huffington Post*, November 5,
2015, http://www.huffingtonpost.com/entry/this-trans-woman-asks
-you-really-want-me-in-the-same-bathroom-as-your-husband
_us_563b997fe4b0411d3070003a.

Office for Victims of Crime, *Responding to Transgender Victims of Sexual Assault* (Washington, DC: US Dept. of Justice, June 2014), http://www.ovc.gov/pubs/forge/sexual_numbers.html.

Sexual Assault Awareness and Prevention Center at the University of Michigan, "Understanding the Perpetrator," https://sapac.umich.edu/article/196, accessed December 19, 2016.

Rebecca J. Stones, "Which Gender Is More Concerned About Transgender Women in Female Bathrooms?," *Gender Issues* (December 19, 2016), doi:10.1007/s12147-016-9181-6.

Transgender Law Center, "Arizona Bathroom Bill Flushed Away—For Now," June 6, 2013, http://transgenderlawcenter.org/archives/8128.

Tim Wildmon, "10 Examples of Men Abusing Target's Dangerous Policy," *The Stand*, blog, American Family Association, September 29, 2016, http://www.afa.net/the-stand/press-releases/2016/09/10-examples-of-men-abusing-targets-dangerous-policy/#.V-ooxnb_PE4.facebook.

MYTH 14: TRANS PEOPLE ARE MENTALLY ILL AND THERAPY CAN CHANGE THEM

American College of Pediatricians, "Gender Ideology Harms Children," http://www.acpeds.org/the-college-speaks/position-statements/gender-ideology-harms-children, updated August 17, 2016.

American Psychiatric Association, *Diagnostic and Statistical Manual of Mental Disorders*, 3rd ed. (Washington, DC: American Psychiatric Association, 1980).

American Psychiatric Association, *Diagnostic and Statistical Manual of Mental Disorders*, 4th ed. (Washington, DC: American Psychiatric Association, 1994).

American Psychiatric Association, *Diagnostic and Statistical Manual of Mental Disorders*, 5th ed. (Washington, DC: American Psychiatric Association, 2013).

L. Bye et al., *California Lesbians, Gays, Bisexuals, and Transgender Tobacco Use Survey—2004* (San Francisco: California Department of Health Services, 2005), http://www.lgbttobacco.org/files/2004%20-%20Bye%20LGBTTobaccoStudy.pdf.

Tamar Carmel and Laura Erickson-Schroth, "Mental Health and the Transgender Population," *Psychiatric Annals* 46, no. 6 (2016): 346–49.

E. Castellano et al., "Quality of Life and Hormones After Sex Reassignment Surgery," *Journal of Endocrinological Investigation* 38, no. 12 (2015): 1373–81, http://doi.org/10.1007/s40618-015-0398-0.

Colin Close, *Affirming Gender, Affirming Lives: A Report of the 2011 Transition Survey* (Santa Rosa, CA: GATE, July 2012), http://www.transstudent.org /Affirming_Gender.pdf.

M. Colizzi et al., "Transsexual Patients' Psychiatric Comorbidity and Positive Effect of Cross-Sex Hormonal Treatment on Mental Health: Results from a Longitudinal Study," *Psychoneuroendocrinology* 39 (2014): 65–73.

A. L. C. de Vries et al., "Young Adult Psychological Outcome After Puberty Suppression and Gender Reassignment," *Pediatrics* 134, no. 4 (2014): 696–704.

Jack Drescher, "Gender Diagnoses in the *DSM* and *ICD*," *Psychiatric Annals* 46, no. 6 (2016): 350–54.

Diane Ehrensaft, "We Trust Kids to Know What Gender They Are," University of California News, May 27, 2015, http://www.universityofcalifornia .edu/news/we-trust-kids-know-what-gender-they-are.

Diane Ehrensaft, "Apples, Oranges, and Fruit Salad: Sorting out Transgender, Gender Non-Conforming, & Nonbinary Children and Youth," *GID Reform* blog, September 23, 2016, https://gidreform.wordpress.com.

Laura Erickson-Schroth and Elizabeth Glaeser, "The Role of Resilience and Resilience Characteristics in Health Promotion," in *Trauma, Resilience, and Health Promotion for LGBT Patients: What Every Healthcare Provider Should Know*, ed. Kristen L. Eckstrand and Jennifer Potter (New York: Springer, 2017).

Fredriksen-Goldsen, et al., *The Aging and Health Report*.

Zach Ford, "Infamous Reparative Therapy Clinic for Transgender Youth Set to Close," *Think Progress*, December 16, 2015, https://thinkprogress.org /infamous-reparative-therapy-clinic-for-transgender-youth-set-to -close-bd4e960519c3#.l5ihpm2xa.

Jaime Grant et al., *National Transgender Discrimination Survey Report on Health and Health Care* (Washington, DC: National Center for Transgender Equality, October 2010), http://www.thetaskforce.org/static _html/downloads/resources_and_tools/ntds_report_on_health.pdf.

Nick Gorton and Hilary Maia Grubb, "General, Sexual, and Reproductive Health," in Erickson-Schroth, *Trans Bodies, Trans Selves*.

Michael L. Hendricks and Rylan J. Testa, "A Conceptual Framework for Clinical Work with Transgender and Gender Nonconforming Clients: An Adaptation of the Minority Stress Model," *Professional Psychology: Research and Practice* 43, no. 5 (October 2012): 460-67, http://dx.doi .org/10.1037/a0029597.

Human Rights Campaign, "The Lies and Dangers of Efforts to Change Sexual Orientation or Gender Identity," http://www.hrc.org/resources/the-lies-and-dangers-of-reparative-therapy, accessed December 23, 2016.

Justin Ling, "Canada's Most Populous Province Just Banned Conversion Therapy for LGBTQ Youth," *Vice*, June 4, 2015, https://news.vice.com/article/canadas-most-populous-province-just-banned-conversion-therapy-for-lgbtq-youth.

E. Lombardi, "Substance Use Treatment Experiences of Transgender/Transsexual Men and Women," *Journal of LGBT Health Research* 3, no. 2 (2007): 37–47.

Paul McHugh, "Transgender Surgery Isn't the Solution," *Wall Street Journal*, June 12, 2014, http://www.wsj.com/articles/paul-mchugh-transgender-surgery-isnt-the-solution-1402615120.

I. H. Meyer, "Prejudice, Social Stress, and Mental Health in Lesbian, Gay, and Bisexual Populations: Conceptual Issues and Research Evidence," *Psychological Bulletin* 129, no. 5 (2003): 674.

M. H. Murad et al., "Hormonal Therapy and Sex Reassignment: A Systematic Review and Meta-Analysis of Quality of Life and Psychosocial Outcomes," *Clinical Endocrinology* 72, no. 2 (2010): 214-31, doi: 10.1111/j.1365-2265.2009.03625.x.

National Alliance on Mental Illness, "LGBTQ."

Olson et al., "Mental Health of Transgender Children Who Are Supported in Their Identities."

Casey Plett, "Zucker's 'Therapy' Mourned Almost Exclusively by Cis People," Harlot Media, April 11, 2016, http://harlot.media/articles/2582/zuckers-therapy-mourned-almost-exclusively-by-cis-people.

C. Ryan et al., "Family Acceptance in Adolescence and the Health of LGBT Adults," *Journal of Child and Adolescent Psychiatric Nursing* 23 (2010): 205–13.

Julia Serano, "Placing Ken Zucker's Clinic in Historical Context," *Whipping Girl*, February 9, 2016, http://juliaserano.blogspot.com/2016/02/placing-ken-zuckers-clinic-in.html.

Michael D. Shear, "Obama Calls for End to 'Conversion' Therapies for Gay and Transgender Youth," *New York Times*, April 8, 2015, http://www.nytimes.com/2015/04/09/us/politics/obama-to-call-for-end-to-conversion-therapies-for-gay-and-transgender-youth.html.

J. M. White Hughto and S. L. Reisner, "A Systematic Review of the Effects of Hormone Therapy on Psychological Functioning and Quality of Life in Transgender Individuals," *Transgender Health* 1, no. 1 (2016): 21–31.

Coleman et al., "Standards of Care for the Health of Transsexual, Transgender, and Gender-Nonconforming People, Version 7."

MYTH 15: GETTING HORMONES AND SURGERY IS EASY

Cecilia Dhejne et al., "An Analysis of All Applications for Sex Reassignment Surgery in Sweden, 1960–2010: Prevalence, Incidence, and
Regrets," *Archives of Sexual Behavior* 43, no. 8 (2014): 1535–45.

Juno Obedin-Maliver et al., "Lesbian, Gay, Bisexual, and Transgender–
Related Content in Undergraduate Medical Education," *Journal of the
American Medical Association (JAMA)* 306, no. 9 (2011): 971–77.

F. Pfaffln and A. Junge, *Sex Reassignment: Thirty Years of International
Follow-Up Studies After SRS—A Comprehensive Review, 1961–1991*, trans.
Roberta B. Jacobson and Alf B. Meier (orig., 1992; Dusseldorf, Ger-
many: Symposion Publishing, 1998), published as a supplement to the
International Journal of Transgenderism, http://web.archive.org/web
/20070503090247/.

MYTH 16: TESTOSTERONE MAKES YOU ANGRY AND ESTROGEN MAKES YOU EMOTIONAL

Colizzi et al., "Transsexual Patients' Psychiatric Comorbidity and Positive
Effect of Cross-Sex Hormonal Treatment on Mental Health."

A. Costantino et al., "A Prospective Study on Sexual Function and Mood
in Female-to-Male Transsexuals During Testosterone Administration
and After Sex Reassignment Surgery," *Journal of Sex and Marital Therapy* 39, no. 4 (2013): 321–35.

Dhejne et al., "An Analysis of All Applications for Sex Reassignment Surgery in Sweden."

G. Heylens et al., "Effects of Different Steps in Gender Reassignment Therapy on Psychopathology: A Prospective Study of Persons with a Gender
Identity Disorder," *Journal of Sexual Medicine* 11, no. 1 (2014): 119–26.

Hughto and Reisner, "A Systematic Review of the Effects of Hormone
Therapy on Psychological Functioning and Quality of Life in Transgender Individuals."

Chiara Manieri et al., "Medical Treatment of Subjects with Gender Identity
Disorder: The Experience in an Italian Public Health Center," *International Journal of Transgenderism* 15, no. 2 (2014): 53–65.

Murad et al., "Hormonal Therapy and Sex Reassignment."

F. Pfafflin and A. Junge, *Sex Reassignment.*

K. Wierckx et al., "Sexual Desire in Female-to-Male Transsexual Persons:
Exploration of the Role of Testosterone Administration," *European
Journal of Endocrinology* 165, no. 2 (2011): 331–37.

K. Wierckx et al., "Sexual Desire in Trans Persons: Associations with Sex Reassignment Treatment," *Journal of Sexual Medicine* 11, no. 1 (2014): 107–18, doi:10.1111/jsm.12365.

MYTH 17: LAWS SUPPORT TRANS PEOPLE

Morgan Bassichis, Alexander Lee, and Dean Spade, "Building an Abolitionist Trans and Queer Movement with Everything We've Got," in *Captive Genders: Trans Embodiment and the Prison Industrial Complex*, ed. Eric A Stanley and Nat Smith (Oakland, CA: AK Press), 15–40.

Julie Hirschfeld Davis and Matt Apuzzo, "U.S. Directs Public Schools to Allow Transgender Access to Restrooms," *New York Times*, May 12, 2016, http://www.nytimes.com/2016/05/13/us/politics/obama-administration-to-issue-decree-on-transgender-access-to-school-restrooms.html.

Anand Kaira, "New ACA Rule Bans Anti-Trans Discrimination in Health Care! What Does This Mean for You?," Transgender Law Center, May 13, 2016, http://transgenderlawcenter.org/archives/12908.

Lambda Legal, "FAQ: Answers to Common Questions about Transgender Workplace Rights," http://www.lambdalegal.org/know-your-rights/transgender/trans-workplace-faq, accessed December 23, 2016.

Michelle Ye Hee Lee, "Does the United States Really Have 5% of the World Population and One Quarter of the World's Prisoners?," *Washington Post*, April 30, 2015, https://www.washingtonpost.com/news/fact-checker/wp/2015/04/30/does-the-united-states-really-have-five-percent-of-worlds-population-and-one-quarter-of-the-worlds-prisoners/.

Mitch Kellaway, "DOJ Tells State Prisons: Denying Trans Inmates Hormone Therapy Is Unconstitutional," *Advocate*, April 8, 2015, http://www.advocate.com/politics/transgender/2015/04/08/doj-tells-state-prisons-denying-trans-inmates-hormone-therapy-uncons.

"Federal Survey: 40% of Transgender Prisoners Are Sexually Abused Each Year," *Advancing Transgender Equality*, blog post, National Center for Transgender Equality, December 18, 2014, https://transgenderequality.wordpress.com/2014/12/18/federal-survey-40-of-transgender-prisoners-are-sexually-abused-each-year/, accessed December 23, 2016.

National Center for Transgender Equality, "Know Your Rights: Medicare," http://www.transequality.org/know-your-rights/medicare, accessed December 23, 2016.

Grant et al., *National Transgender Discrimination Survey Report on Health and Health Care*.

National Center for Transgender Equality, "Transgender People and the Social Security Administration," June 2013, http://www.transequality .org/sites/default/files/docs/kyr/SSAResource_June2013.pdf.

National Center for Transgender Equality, "Understanding the Passport Gender Change Policy," March 2014, http://www.transequality.org /sites/default/files/docs/kyr/passports_2014.pdf.

Brandon Ellington Patterson, "Justice Department Takes Steps to Protect Transgender Prisoners," *Mother Jones*, March 25, 2016, http://www .motherjones.com/politics/2016/03/doj-trans-inmate-guidelines.

Paige St. John, "In a First, California Agrees to Pay for Transgender Inmate's Sex Reassignment," *Los Angeles Times*, August 10, 2015, http:// www.latimes.com/local/california/la-me-inmate-transgender -20150810-story.html.

Dean Spade, *Normal Life: Administrative Violence, Critical Trans Politics, and the Limits of Law* (Brooklyn, NY: South End Press, 2011), 138.

Matthew Rosenberg, "Transgender People Will Be Able to Serve Openly in Military," *New York Times*, June 30, 2016, http://www.nytimes.com /2016/07/01/us/transgender-military.html.

MYTH 18: TRANS PEOPLE HAVE EXISTED THROUGHOUT TIME

Genny Beemyn, "US History," in Erickson-Schroth, *Trans Bodies, Trans Selves*.

David Cauldwell, "Psychopathia Transsexualis," *Sexology* 16 (1949): 274–80.

John D'Emilio, "Capitalism and Gay Identity," in *Families in the U.S.: Kinship and Domestic Politics*, ed. Karen V. Hansen and Anita Ilta Garey (Philadelphia: Temple University Press, 1998), 131–41.

Havelock Ellis and John Addington Symonds, *Sexual Inversion* (London: Wilson and Macmillan, 1897).

Rhys Ernst, *We've Been Around*, documentary series, 2016, http://www .wevebeenaround.com/episodes.

Leslie Feinberg, *Transgender Warriors: Making History from Joan of Arc to Dennis Rodman* (Boston: Beacon Press, 1996).

Michel Foucault, *The History of Sexuality: An Introduction*, vol. 1, trans. Robert Hurley (New York: Vintage, 1990).

Magnus Hirschfeld, *Transvestites: The Erotic Drive to Cross-Dress*, trans. Michael Lombardi-Nash (Buffalo, NY: Prometheus Books, 1991).

Richard von Krafft-Ebing, *Psychopathia Sexualis: With Especial Reference to the Antipathic Sexual Instinct: A Medico-Forensic Study*, trans. and with an introduction by F. S. Klaf (orig., 1921; New York: Arcade, 1965).

Susan Stryker, *Transgender History* (Berkeley, CA: Seal Press, 2008).

Karl Heinrich Ulrichs, *The Riddle of "Man-Manly" Love: The Pioneering Work on Male Homosexuality*, vol. 1, trans. Michael A. Lombardi-Nash (orig., 1864; Buffalo, NY: Prometheus, 1994), 197.

David Valentine, *Imagining Transgender: An Ethnography of a Category* (Durham, NC: Duke University Press, 2007).

Ralph Werther (as Earl Lind), *Autobiography of an Androgyne* (orig., 1918; New York: Arno, 1975).

MYTH 19: CERTAIN CULTURES UNIVERSALLY EMBRACE TRANS PEOPLE

Beja, "A Letter to White People Using the Term 'Two Spirit,'" White Noise Collective, May 18, 2015, http://www.conspireforchange.org/?p=2283.

Dan Bilefsky, "Sworn to Virginity and Living as Men in Albania," *New York Times*, June 23, 2008, http://www.nytimes.com/2008/06/23/world/europe/23iht-virgins.4.13927949.html.

Peter A. Jackson, "Tolerant but Unaccepting: The Myth of a Thai 'Gay Paradise,'" in *Genders & Sexualities in Modern Thailand*, ed. Peter A. Jackson and Nerida M. Cook (Chiang Mai, Thailand: Silkworm Books, 1999), 227–42.

Homa Khaleeli, "Hijra: India's Third Gender Claims Its Place in Law," *Guardian*, April 16, 2014, https://www.theguardian.com/society/2014/apr/16/india-third-gender-claims-place-in-law.

Dominique Mosbergen, "Two-Faced Thailand: The Ugly Side of 'Asia's Gay Capital,'" *Huffington Post*, October 20, 2015, http://www.huffingtonpost.com/entry/lgbt-thailand_us_5616472ee4bodbb8000d30a6.

Native Out, "Two Spirit 101," http://nativeout.com/twospirit-rc/two-spirit-101/, accessed December 23, 2016.

Valentine Pasquesoone, "7 Countries Giving Transgender People Fundamental Rights the US Still Won't," *Identities.Mic*, April 9, 2014, https://mic.com/articles/87149/7-countries-giving-transgender-people-fundamental-rights-the-u-s-still-won-t#.vVz2U5Moc.

Preeti Sharma, "Historical Background and Legal Status of Third Gender in Indian Society," *International Journal of Research in Economics & Social Sciences* 2, no. 12 (December 2012): 64–71, https://web.archive.org/web/20140203031618/http://www.euroasiapub.org/IJRESS/dec2012/7.pdf.

Will Roscoe, "Who Are the Two Spirits?," http://www.willsworld.org/twospiritq-a.html, accessed December 9, 2016.

Patrick Winn, "This Gym in Thailand Is Staffed Exclusively by Transgender Men," *Global Post*, June 15, 2016, http://www.pri.org/stories/2016-06-15/gym-thailand-staffed-exclusively-transgender-men.

Antonia Young, *Women Who Become Men: Albanian Sworn Virgins* (Oxford, UK: Berg Publishers, 2000).

MYTH 20: TRANS PEOPLE AND FEMINISTS DON'T GET ALONG

Emma Allen, "Unpacking Transphobia*," *Radical Women*, June 2013, http://www.radicalwomen.org/transphobia.shtml.

Stephan L. Cohen, *The Gay Liberation Youth Movement in New York: "An Army of Lovers Cannot Fail"* (New York: Routledge, 2007).

Michelle Goldberg, "What Is a Woman? The Dispute Between Radical Feminism and Transgenderism," *New Yorker*, August 4, 2014, http://www.newyorker.com/magazine/2014/08/04/woman-2.

Michelle Goldberg, "The Trans Women Who Say That Trans Women Aren't Women," *Slate*, December 9, 2015, http://www.slate.com/articles/double_x/doublex/2015/12/gender_critical_trans_women_the_apostates_of_the_trans_rights_movement.single.html.

Emi Koyama, "The Transfeminist Manifesto," July 26, 2001, http://eminism.org/readings/pdf-rdg/tfmanifesto.pdf.

Robin Morgan, *Going Too Far: The Personal Chronicle of a Feminist* (New York: Random House, 1977).

Janice Raymond, *Transsexual Empire: The Making of the She-Male* (Boston: Beacon Press, 1979).

Julia Serano, *Whipping Girl: A Transsexual Woman on Sexism and the Scapegoating of Femininity* (Berkeley: Seal Press, 2007).

Roey Thorpe, "Where Have All the Butches Gone?," *Pride*, July 15, 2015, http://www.pride.com/lifestyle/2013/09/05/op-ed-where-have-all-butches-gone.

MYTH 21: THE LGBTQ+ COMMUNITY IS UNITED

Morgan, Lee, and Spade, "Building an Abolitionist Trans and Queer Movement with Everything We've Got."

Arthur Bell, *Dancing the Gay Lib Blues: A Year in the Homosexual Liberation Movement* (New York: Simon and Schuster, 1971).

Cohen, *The Gay Liberation Youth Movement in New York*.

Martin B. Duberman, *Stonewall* (New York: Plume, 1994).

The Lesbian Avengers, "About the Lesbian Avengers," http://www.lesbianavengers.com/about/history.shtml, accessed December 23, 2016.

The Lesbian Avengers, "Trans Activists Storm Stage at Creating Change" Bilerico Project, http://bilerico.lgbtqnation.com/2015/02/trans_activists_storm_stage_at_creating_change.php, accessed December 23, 2016.

Maddie, "Queers for Economic Justice Closes Its Doors Thanks to Lack of
Economic Justice," *Autostraddle*, February 24, 2014, http://www.auto
straddle.com/queers-for-economic-justice-closes-its-doors-thanks
-to-lack-of-economic-justice-224520/.

David Marcus, "Exclusive: Gay Man Explains His Petition to Drop the T in
LGBT," *Federalist*, November 9, 2015, http://thefederalist.com/2015
/11/09/exclusive-gay-man-explains-his-petition-to-drop-the-t
-in-lgbt/.

Mattilda Bernstein Sycamore, ed., *That's Revolting! Queer Strategies for
Resisting Assimilation* (Brooklyn, NY: Soft Skull Press, 2008).